The Origins of Materialism

) materialism, a Western
intellectual development!?
See Diop, African
Philosophy, also Mbiti,
Mooselo, and Mucimbe!

The Origins of Materialism

The evolution of a scientific view of the world

George Novack

Pathfinder

New York   London   Montreal   Sydney

For Evelyn

ISBN 0-87348-022-8
Library of Congress Catalog Card Number 76-160511
Manufactured in the United States of America

First edition, 1965
Sixth printing, 1995

Cover design: Eric Simpson
Cover illustration: Cup from Greece, sixth century B.C., depicting
the weighing and storing of commodities

Pathfinder
410 West Street, New York, NY 10014, U.S.A.
Fax: (212) 727-0150 • CompuServe: 73321,414
Internet: pathfinder@igc.apc.org

Pathfinder distributors around the world:
Australia (and Asia and the Pacific):
        Pathfinder, 19 Terry St., Surry Hills, Sydney, N.S.W. 2010
        Postal address: P.O. Box K879, Haymarket, N.S.W. 2000
Canada:
        Pathfinder, 4851 rue St-Denis, Montreal, Quebec, H2J 2L4
Iceland:
        Pathfinder, Klapparstíg 26, 2d floor, 101 Reykjavik
        Postal address: P. Box 233, 121 Reykjavik
New Zealand:
        Pathfinder, La Gonda Arcade, 203 Karangahape Road, Auckland
        Postal address: P.O. Box 8730, Auckland
Sweden:
        Pathfinder, Vikingagatan 10, S-113 42, Stockholm
United Kingdom (and Europe, Africa except South Africa, and Middle East):
        Pathfinder, 47 The Cut, London, SE1 8LL
United States (and Caribbean, Latin America, and South Africa):
        Pathfinder, 410 West Street, New York, NY 10014

Contents

Foreword

This book deals with the first steps in the development of the materialist conception of the world. It is a sequel and supplement to an earlier work, *An Introduction to the Logic of Marxism,* which outlined the main ideas of the dialectical method of thought but made only incidental reference to the materialist foundations of the Marxist outlook. Here attention is centered upon the materialist side of Marxism.

In the first chapter the fundamental positions of materialism and idealism are presented in schematic form. These two viewpoints on the nature of reality, which were first projected by the Greeks, mark out the boundaries of philosophic thought. Today they stand in outright opposition to each other. But it has taken 2,500 years to work out the full ramifications of these philosophical positions, counterpose their essential differences clearly and sharply, and expose their total incompatibility.

It has taken no less time to bring the outlook of materialism to its present clarity and comprehensiveness. One of the principal propositions of dialectical materialism asserts that nothing can be fully understood unless and until its entire course of development has been disclosed and grasped. This demand of the Marxist method has to be applied to materialism itself.

The second chapter proposes to show that the materialist attitude is not primarily a matter of theory but of fact proved by practice. It is first of all solidly rooted in the circumstances of everyday life, in the interactions between people and their natural environment and in their interconnections with one another. Materialism arises from the common practices and productive activities of mankind. But there was, and remains to this day, an immense gap between unreflecting behavior based upon unconscious materialist premises and a generalized theory corresponding to that practice and verified by scientific procedures. Toiling mankind went through hundreds of thousands of years to create the historical conditions required to bridge the gap between the naive realism of primitive life and the first formulation of a distinctively materialist method and world outlook in conceptual terms.

The bulk of this book traces the evolution of materialist theorizing from its emergence among the Ionian Greeks through its elaboration in Graeco-Roman society.

This should form the first section of a broader work which would go on to discuss the reasons for the 1,200-year exile of materialism from European thought following its Mediterranean birth; its transmission to the West through Moslem and Jewish thinkers; its fugitive appearances here and there during the Middle Ages; its revival in Western Europe as part of the rise of bourgeois society; and its career in the modern world culminating in the rounded development it has received in the teachings of Marxism.

Materialism cannot claim to have burst upon the world full-grown, like a religious revelation. It has been the product of a prolonged historical development in the field of ideas. First fashioned by the Greeks, it passed through complex processes of intellectual labor by many keen minds. Modern materialism is the outcome, the valid residue, of several thousand years of conscious inquiry into the most fundamental and far-reaching aspects of the universe we inhabit and our ways of knowing them.

To understand the most up-to-date means of agricultural production, with their tremendous powers, it is necessary to go far back to the crudest implements of our savage ancestors and then follow their developments step by step. The British Museum of Science in London houses a chronological series of agricultural implements used to prepare the soil for planting seeds. The exhibit starts with the digging sticks and hoes of the savages, moves forward to the animal-drawn plow and harrow, and ends with the tractor. The primitive digging stick, taken from the root or branch of a tree and sharpened to a point, is far removed from the power-driven metal machinery on today's farms. Yet it was the first in the sequence of tools which has revolutionized food and fiber production and elevated civilization to its present eminence.

These are implements of labor which, although proceeding from collective activity and individual thought, are material things used in the productive process. Philosophies are combinations of ideas which, while referring to objective realities, are essentially mental in character. However, the tools of thought, the concepts, used for intellectual production in the field of philosophy, have origins similar to the material means of production that men fabricate. These concepts have been created in accord with the evolution of man's productive powers and out of his changing social relations. The first general ideas of a materialist character were very crude and hazy. But they contained the seeds of further growth and from them have come the more precise and versatile tools of thought, the more correct concepts, the clear and comprehensive formulations provided by the dialectical materialism of Marxism.

When we analyze the course of materialism from its beginnings among the Greeks up to today, we can distinguish three main stages in its unfolding and three fundamental types of materialist thought bound up with them. These are:

1. Ancient materialism, starting with Thales in the 6th Century B.C. and culminating with Lucretius in the 1st Century B.C.

2. Bourgeois materialism which originated in the 16th Century in Italy and concluded with Feuerbach in the 19th Century.

3. Dialectical materialism, the outlook of the indus-

trial working class, created by Marx and Engels in the middle of the 19th Century and advanced since their death largely through their German and Russian disciples.

The first phase, from the naturalism of the Ionians to the mechanical atomism of Lucretius, brought out the basic principles of materialism but in elementary and restricted ways. The ancient materialists announced the themes which their successors were to elaborate. Both the dialectical and the mechanical aspects of their thought were set forth—but neither received a well-rounded development.

As society and science marched forward, materialism grew more complex in its structure and richer in the content of its discoveries and thought determinations. The second stage of materialism, which grew out of the rise of capitalism, was predominantly mechanical in its world outlook and rigidly metaphysical in its mode of thought. Although the present form of materialism, associated with revolutionary socialism, acknowledges the validity of mechanics in its proper sphere, it is thoroughly evolutionary in its approach and dialectical in its method.

Within each of these extended periods of its development, materialism had many shadings and went through many meanderings. Materialism in antiquity, for example, passed through three major stages, each of them linked with a specific period in the history of Mediterranean society: the Ionian School of the 6th and 5th Centuries; the original Atomists of the 5th and 4th Centuries; and the Epicureans who flourished from the 4th Century B.C. to the 2nd Century A.D.

There were also transitional trends such as the currents of materialist thought among the Arabs who preserved some of the teachings of antiquity and thus prepared the rebirth of materialism in Western Europe, or like Feuerbach's work which served as a bridge between the mechanical materialism of the 18th Century and dialectical materialism. But the three traditions mentioned are the historically dominant types which followed one another in the evolution of the materialist conception of reality.

The historian of materialism should try to show the social and scientific conditions which produced these three stages of materialist philosophy; the historical changes which transformed, outmoded and elevated them; and the identities and differences between them. One of the objectives of scientific study is to demonstrate, contrary to the skeptics, that history, including the history of philosophy, makes sense and has positive and progressive results. Despite its aberrations, repetitions and relapses, philosophy has had a logical line of growth which has been governed by the changing conditions of social and intellectual life in the Western world. So has the history of materialism which has been the most fruitful product of that growth and provides the best guide to understanding the universe around us.

This work does not deal with the whole stream of philosophy but concentrates upon one current in it; the principal stages in the early evolution of materialism and the decisive features of each stage. Even this account has limitations. It is restricted to Western philosophy. As the horizon of ancient history has widened, it has dawned upon the West that China and India produced parallel initiatives in rational speculation, logic and materialist thought. In *The First Philosophers* George Thomson has recently given a rewarding comparative study from the Marxist standpoint of such beginnings in China and Greece.

But these Eastern lines of philosophical pioneering have to be left unconsidered. They would take us too far afield from our principal purpose which is to follow the progress of materialism from its first appearance to its present fulfillment. For special historical reasons, the promising buds of philosophy in the East did not ripen and bear such fruit as in the West. Only the materialist tendencies and traditions in Western Europe have had a sustained course of development, despite interruptions and divagations. They alone culminated in the scientific school of Marxism, the highest form of materialism, which has become an indispensable acquisition of contemporary world culture.

This is a study of materialism in its evolution rather than a record of the materialists. Although the two are inseparable, they are not identical. Materialism as a world outlook has had an objective development greater than any one of its exponents, however profound their understandings and important their individual contributions.

But this is not a complete history of materialism in all its windings and complications. Such a detailed study may be necessary for scholars; it cannot serve as an introduction to the subject. Of course, socialist scholars should strive to acquire a profound knowledge

of the entire range of philosophy. But that task is
different from the present one which is to set forth
the main findings in this field as simply and clearly
as possible.

There are special obstacles in the way of accom-
plishing either of these aims. Philosophy has largely
been studied and its history written not by materialists but by idealistically-inclined scholars. These authors have often disregarded, minimized or distorted
the ideas and roles of the materialists in the making
of Western thought. Others, directed by a purely rationalistic view of the history of philosophy, have given
extremely inadequate   accounts of the materialist
thinkers, severing the development of their ideas from
the specific historical circumstances and social antagonisms which nurtured and formed them.

This unsatisfactory state of affairs is emphasized
by the scarcity of treatises on the history of materialism. There are many histories of philosophy but very
few general treatments of its materialist expressions.
To be sure, numerous excellent expositions of the
fundamental ideas of materialism and separate aspects of its development have been written. But the
only comprehensive account of materialism in English
I am familiar with is the three-volume *History of
Materialism* originally delivered as a course of lec-
tures at the University of Bonn and first published in
1865 by the German professor of philosophy Frederick
Lange. This work, while still useful, is pitifully defi-
cient and misleading.

Lange himself was not a materialist; he was a semi-
idealist of the Kantian school who attempted through

his history to correct the shortcomings of materialism as he understood—or, more correctly, misunderstood—them. Marx and Engels knew his work and criticized it sharply. Lenin correctly characterized it as a "falsified" history of materialism. Yet no better has been written to supersede it almost a century later.

The indispensable guides to understanding the doctrines of materialism and its history are contained in the works of the founders of Marxism from their earliest writings on philosophical questions in the 1840's to Engels' final letters on historical materialism in 1895. The best expositions of Marxist philosophy are still to be found in the writings of Plekhanov. Plekhanov educated the entire generation of Russian Marxists who led the Bolshevik Revolution and all his essays on theoretical problems still sparkle with insight and information.

His most extensive work is *In Defense of Materialism* which Lenin praised as "a remarkably logical and valuable exposition of dialectical materialism." This starts with the French materialists of the second half of the 18th Century and concludes with an explanation of the views of dialectical materialism. That served Plekhanov's polemical purposes at the time against the Russian subjectivist school of sociology. But it restricted the scope of his treatment to the culminating episodes in the development of bourgeois materialism in the 18th and 19th Centuries and its passage from the high points of that materialism over to scientific socialism.

The English Marxists, headed by George Thomson and Benjamin Farrington, heavily influenced by the official Communist movement, have made notable contributions to our understanding of materialism in antiquity which I have drawn upon. Farrington has illuminated the influence of technology upon Greek science; Thomson has set forth the roles of commodity production, money circulation and the democratic revolution in the formation of Greek philosophy.

But there remains an unfilled need for a connected account of the whole span and sequence of materialist thought. This is a small installment on that account in a field where so much has still to be explored and charted.

*   *   *

One other noteworthy difficulty stands in the way of setting forth the development of materialism. Philosophizing is a highly specialized function of social activity; it is only one aspect of the complex of civilized culture. Materialism, one of the two major trends of philosophy, has coexisted and pre-existed in other forms than that of abstract philosophical theory.

Materialism flows from the practical activities of society and pervades many departments of human life. In fact, a generalized statement of a materialist outlook and a correspondingly well-defined method of procedure is much rarer than concrete materialistic attitudes manifested in politics, law, manners and morals, craftsmanship, the arts and sciences. The formulation of a materialist philosophy comes about as the highest expression of such tendencies in other spheres of vital action.

The urge for its expression is so powerful that materialism can even be banished from official philosophy and still assert itself elsewhere. Because of its heretical implications materialism was anathema, for example, in medieval Europe where the theology of the Catholic Church held philosophy captive. Yet the materialist impulse, blocked from direct formulation in theoretical conclusions, welled out through other channels.

It was manifested in the irreverence toward the clergy expressed artistically in the French popular tales called *fabliaux,* in the wood carvings on choir stalls and gargoyles on cathedrals, in the literary works of Boccaccio and Chaucer which made fun of priests and depicted monks as fornicators, liars, gluttons, drunkards, idlers and hypocrites.

Chaucer's *Canterbury Tales* exemplifies how the materialist devil creeps in despite official bans. Materialism was as remote from Chaucer's intentions as it was absent from the philosophy of 14th Century England. At the end of his poem the devout Catholic asks Christ in his great mercy "to forgive his sins," among them his "writings of worldly vanities."

However Chaucer's critical attitude toward high dignitaries of the Church in his *Tales* betrayed a latent materialism. This comes out most plainly in his portraits of the Nunne Prioresse and the Monk-Prior in the *Prologue.* The poet depicts the Nunne Prioresse as a lady preoccupied with such earthly things as cultivated speech, fine manners, fashionable clothes, gay jewelry beneath the veneer of her ecclesiastical vocation. Her rosary is tricked in green with a golden broach inscribed: *Love Conquers All.* He slyly insinuates that this motto is not focused exclusively upon heavenly adorations.

His "fat and personable" Monk and greedy Friar have equally worldly concerns. Chaucer exposes the gap between the real features of these clerical personages and the pretentions of their offices. And he accentuates the contrast through his portrait of the poor Parson who not only taught Christ's creed but "followed it himself before."

The point is that the poet's realistic observation of the social types around him in medieval England was animated by an unconscious but no less influential materialist spirit. The criticism of the Church hierarchy, though far from formulation in general terms, was nevertheless present in the penetrating vision of the creative artist. He, together with Langland and Wyclif, heralded the protests against the abuses of that omnipresent feudal institution which were to gather force from many sides and explode in the unrestrainable outburst of anti-Catholic thought and feeling which tore the British Church from Rome less than two centuries later.

Descending from the more rarefied regions of religion and literature in the Middle Ages, we can discern an even more powerful outburst of materialist sentiment in the political arena of North America five centuries later. Tom Paine was not a poet; he was the principal propagandist for the first successful colonial revolution of modern times. He was neither a Catholic nor an atheist but a deist, that is, a Protestant rationalist. But his religious beliefs stopped short at "the divine origins and right of kings."

In order to justify the colonists' struggle for independence and the rightness of republicanism, he was impelled not only to ridicule and reject the godlike pretentions of the monarchists but to turn them upside down. He castigated the role of King George III as a spawn of the devil and a curse upon mankind. This was a materialist assault upon the theological supports of royalism, inspired by the political aims of the revolutionary cause.

Similar contradictions between anti-materialist theory and materialist practice can be observed closer to home in our own time among the working people. A religious-minded worker, for example, can go to church Sunday and nod assent to the preacher's talk that all men are brothers, God is their father, and the things of this earth count for nothing compared to the rewards of a heavenly hereafter. The next day he can belie all these pious sentiments by going on strike for a raise in wages against a boss who may belong to the same denomination. He will fight scabs and police and carry on the class struggle very materialistically in his own way. His most general ideas can be completely at odds with all these practical actions in defense of his material welfare.

As we see, materialist practice does not always march in step with materialist thinking. Their relations have been complex and often contradictory throughout civilization. But in these pages we are mostly concerned with studying materialism as it has gained expression in its most generalized and self-conscious form through the philosophers from Thales to Marx.

*   *   *

Why has the history of materialism been so neglected and distorted? The materialist philosophy was born in opposition to the archaic religious outlook of an agricultural aristocracy by the new forces of a commercial slave society. It has had to contend for "living space" against conservative master classes ever since.

In Greece, not only materialism but the mere exercise of methodical reasoning, directed as it had to be against old religious ideas and sanctified customs and institutions, was dangerous. Many Greek philosophers suffered persecution, were expelled from their communities, and even put to death for their teachings. In the Athens of Pericles, Anaxagoras was condemned for irreligion and forced to flee for having said that the sun was a "glowing mass of stone" and the moon was of earthly nature. Didn't the priesthood teach that the sun and the moon were divine beings and wasn't religion one of the means for holding the masses in check?

It was even more perilous to profess materialist ideas in the Middle Ages under penalty of being condemned for heresy like Roger Bacon, excommunicated from the Church or killed. Such was the fate inflicted on Giordano Bruno as late as the 17th Century.

Materialist-minded thinkers were hounded and their ideas anathematized throughout the bourgeois epoch. Hundreds of cases could be cited from the expulsion of Descartes from France through Spinoza's excommunication from the Jewish community of Amsterdam to the attacks upon Hobbes and Joseph Priestley in England. Not all of these persecuted philosophers were thoroughgoing materialists. But there was enough of a materialist bent in their criticisms of the prevailing religious and idealist doctrines to render them suspect of unorthodoxy and susceptible to punishment.

Up to our time materialist thinkers and their adherents have almost always and everywhere been in a minority. Some have been forced to lead a hole-and-corner existence and often to withhold the full implications of their ideas. They have been the oppressed tendency in the field of philosophy. However extensive its influence has been at times in certain departments, the materialist outlook has never yet ruled society or the intellectual world as a whole. Nevertheless, the ideas of the materialist scholars and scientists have been among the greatest motive forces of ideological and scientific progress. They have inspired epoch-making achievements in natural science from the broaching of the atomic hypothesis by the Greeks to Darwin's theory of organic evolution.

Despite all this, the materialist viewpoint is still unpopular throughout the Western world, and not least in the United States. Materialism is disfavored not only because it is the principal theoretical weapon against supernaturalism, spiritualism and obscurantism of all kinds. It is so vehemently fought nowadays because the materialist philosophy has become so closely associated with the Socialist movement and Marxism, with the struggles of the workers for liberation from capitalism, with political opposition to the established order.

The struggle between materialism and its opponents which began over 2,500 years ago is still being waged around us. The defenders of capitalism from the universities and churches to the agencies of mass propaganda exert persistent efforts to ward off the penetration of materialist thinking. Here is one typical instance.

The Luce publication, *Life,* the most widely circulated magazine in the United States, is one of the most vigilant participants in the anti-materialist crusade. In 1956 it published a series on *The Epic of Man* which presented the latest findings of science on the origins of civilization. It was impossible to make such a report without undermining, at least by implication, orthodox Christianity. If, as the theory of evolution undeniably demonstrates, mankind rose up out of the animal kingdom, then what credence can be given to Adam and Eve and similar fables of man's divine parentage?

The editors hastened to steer their readers away from any materialist heresy. "The materialist cosmogony," they wrote, "has proven just as unsatisfactory as a literal reading of Genesis, or as Ptolemy's earth-centered welkin, or as the clock-work universe of Newton. And the secret of man's origin and purpose on this planet remains no more and no less mysterious than before." All the conclusions of science, that is to say, tell us nothing more than the Israelite tribes knew about the development of the world and the destiny of mankind!

Having thus disposed of "the materialist cosmogony"—and obliterated the results of science in the bargain—the editors point to the emergence and activity of "conscience" as the decisive proof of man's divine nature. They counterpose eternal morality to the conclusions of modern science based upon the method of materialism. The theoretical arguments of these apologists for the existence of God are as weak as their financial resources and influence are immense.

But one thing is plain. These defenders of religion and capitalism regard materialism as the main ideological enemy to be overcome even at the cost of scientific suicide. These brains at work in skyscrapers fall into line with the adversaries of materialism in ancient Greece, the heresy-hunters of Catholic Europe, and the Baptist bumpkins who tried to ban the teachings of Darwinism in Tennessee decades ago.

The issues between the materialists and anti-materialists have immense practical importance and are far from being settled in real life. This gives our theoretical study its social and political purpose.

In this prolonged and unfinished contest for supremacy between materialism and anti-materialism, science and religion, enlightenment and obscurantism, there is no doubt which will eventually be victorous. Although materialism does not command the field in philosophy or in everyday affairs, on the historical scale it has been gaining and consolidating its ground. It has rich traditions, an ever-growing content and the most diversified applications. It operates today upon much firmer foundations than in the past and has far keener weapons with which to combat its adversaries and solve the problems of science and society.

Materialism receives constant confirmation from the onward march and verified results of technology, the sciences and the developments of industry. It is further fortified by the progress of the class struggle

and the successes of the international workers movement. It derives the most powerful social support and
fresh sources of replenishment from the activities of
the masses in their quest for a better life.

But its biggest battles lie ahead. As in its infancy,
materialism has still to contend for its rightful place
as the outlook of emancipated humanity. Its definitive triumph in the domain of thought is still to
come. May this introduction to its early history help
bring that conquest closer.

George Novack

The Origins of Materialism

I. Materialism Versus Idealism

EVERY PHILOSOPHY HAS DEALT
with two questions: what does reality consist of and
how does it originate? And, after the earliest Greeks,
every philosopher has had to answer the further question: how is reality known? The answers given to these
fundamental questions have determined the nature of
the philosophy and the position of the philosopher.

Almost from the beginning of philosophy there have
been two principal viewpoints on these problems: the
materialist and the idealist. In his pioneering *History
of Philosophy* Hegel declared that "throughout all
time there has only been one Philosophy, the contemporary differences of which constitute the necessary
aspects of the one principal." To be sure, in distinction from other forms of intellectual activity the function of philosophizing has maintained certain common features which give it continuity from the Greeks
to the present day. But this process of generalizing

thought has been at bottom a unity of divergent, and ultimately opposing, ways of rationally explaining the universe. The materialist method stands at one pole; the idealist at the other.

What are the essential principles of materialism which mark it off from all other tendencies in philosophy? What are its distinctive features which enable us to recognize a materialist thinker and to classify a person as reasoning along materialist lines? Let us list them in a very summary manner.

1. The basic proposition of materialism refers to the nature of reality, regardless of the existence of mankind. It states that matter is the primordial substance, the essence, of reality. Everything comes from matter and its movements and is based upon matter. This thought is expressed in the phrase: "Mother Nature." This signifies in materialist terms that nature is the ultimate source of everything in the universe from the galactic systems to the most intimate feelings and boldest thoughts of *homo sapiens*.

2. The second aspect of materialism covers the relations between matter and mind. According to materialism, matter produces mind and mind never exists apart from matter. Mind is the highest product of material development and animal organization and the most complex form of human activity.

3. This means that nature exists independently of mind but that no mind can exist apart from matter. The material world existed long before mankind or any thinking being came into existence. As Feuerbach said: "The true relation of thought to Being is this; Being is subject, thought is predicate. Thought

springs from Being, but Being does not spring
from thought."

4. This precludes the existence of any God, gods,
spirits, souls or other immaterial entities which are
alleged to direct or influence the operations of nature,
society and the inner man.

These are the elementary principles of the materialist outlook. By these signs shall you know a materialist or conversely, a non-materialist, whether or not
that person knows what kind of thinker he really is.

What the materialist principles signify can be further
clarified by contrasting them with a quite different
way of interpreting the world: the idealist philosophy.
One of the dialectical modes of explanation is to show
how a thing is related to its own opposite. For example,
to understand what a female is also involves knowing
what makes a male and how he functions in the cycle
of reproduction. If we want to find out what a capitalist is, we have to know the makeup and development of the wage-worker as well. Only then can we
comprehend the essential nature of the capitalist system which is based upon the relations between these
two interdependent yet antagonistic social classes.

The philosophical opposite of materialism is idealism. These two modes of thought reciprocally define
and limit each other in the province of philosophy.
Therefore, unless we know what idealism is, we cannot fully understand the positions of materialism, and
vice versa.

What does idealism (that is, consistent idealism)
maintain?

1. The basic element of reality is not matter but

mind or spirit. Everything else, in the last analysis, comes from mind or spirit and depends upon its operations.

2. Mind generates material things; behind or before the material world lurks the spirit or mind creating it. Nature may be the mother but there is a God-Father who transcends her.

3. Thus mind or spirit exists before and apart from matter. Spirit is the abiding reality; matter no more than a passing phase or illusion.

4. Mind or spirit is identical with or emanates from the divine, or at least leaves open the possibility of supernatural existence, power and interference.

It should be noted that the basic propositions of these two types of thought are absolutely opposed to each other. One must be right and the other wrong. Both cannot be correct. Whoever maintains consistently the position of the one is inescapably led to conclusions exactly contrary to the other.

Materialism and idealism are the two main tendencies, lines, camps in the field of philosophy, just as the capitalist and working classes are the two principal and decisive social forces in contemporary society. This does not mean that there are no other viewpoints in philosophy. In fact, the history of philosophy exhibits many combinations of ideas and methods which occupy a spectrum of positions between these extremes. Although such shadings of thought cannot be unconditionally grouped under either clear-cut category, their positions can be appraised only by reference to them.

Let us give three examples of these intermediate and

amorphous types of philosophizing. There are ag-
nostics who cannot decide whether an external reality
actually exists apart from ourselves and whether it
is possible to know it. They remain suspended between materialism and idealism, in so far as they
remain agnostic.

Closely associated with them is the theory of knowledge devised by the famous German philosopher Kant.
He taught that "things-in-themselves" existed as objective realities. This was in accord with materialism.
But then he stated that humans could never reach or
know them; all we could know were phenomena or
"things as they appeared to us." This conclusion shoved
Kant back among the idealists.

Many American pragmatists refuse to take a firm
stand on whether or not nature exists independently
of human experience. They are not sure whether experience necessarily arises out of nature and after it,
or whether nature emerges from experience. These
wobblers give all sorts of evasive answers when confronted with this alternative. Although such pragmatists claim to have overcome the opposition between
the materialist and idealist standpoints, they actually
dodge the decisive issues between them in the theory
of knowledge.

All these types of thinking are confused and inconsistent in respect to the fundamental problems posed
by the nature of reality and the theory of knowledge.
When their adherents are pressed against the wall
and obliged to abandon their indefiniteness on these
key questions, they usually end up in alignment with
idealism.

In addition to philosophers who hold essentially eclectic views, we shall meet many thinkers who deserve to be classified among the materialists or idealists because the chief content of their thought proceeds in the one direction or the other, even though their positions on a number of subsidiary points exhibit contrary tendencies.

But we shall be able to analyze and understand all such complex and inconsistent formations in the history of philosophy only if we firmly grasp the characteristic ideas of the decisive opponents: materialism and idealism. These two viewpoints do not exhaust the field of philosophy. But they dominate it. They reciprocally determine not only the main course of its development but the real positions of the schools oscillating between them. They provide the guiding lines which enable us to make our way surely through the maze of philosophical opinions and controversy and not get lost.

The *elementary* principles of materialism have been the same from their first appearance in antiquity to the present day. But the history of materialism has not been the record of a dull repetition of a set of abstract principles which sprang forth fully-grown and were then periodically rediscovered and reasserted in their pristine form. Materialism has passed through a process of genuine growth from the first crude formulations of its essential propositions through its subsequent ramifications to its latest presentation. Materialist philosophy has not only changed its forms but considerably diversified its content and amplified its scope from one stage of its advancement to the next.

Extremely varied superstructures have been built upon the philosophical premises of materialism during the past 2,500 years. The materialism of one epoch displays marked differences from the materialism of another. There are, for example, pronounced differences between the naive evolutionary naturalism of the Milesians of the 6th Century B.C. and the complex mechanical atomism of Lucretius in the 1st Century A.D. Even within the Atomist school itself there are distinct differences; the Lucretian interpretation of Atomism contains many novel observations which are lacking in Democritus and has lopped off some dead branches of ideas.

The dissimilarities between ancient and modern schools of materialist thought are still greater. All materialists have held that matter in motion is the basic reality. But at different times they have put forward different conceptions of matter, different conceptions of motion, and different views of their interconnections.

Consider, for example, the following four definitions of motion, two in ancient and two in modern times. To the Ionians the chief property of material movement consisted in the manner of its coming into being and passing away. The Atomists stressed the displacement of material particles in the void, or empty space.

The bourgeois materialists made the simple mechanical motion of masses and their external impact into the keystone of their world conception, reducing all other modes of motion to that one. Finally, the dialectical materialists have a far more complex and correct definition of motion as the process of universal transformation in which matter acquires the most diversified qualities of motion from the mechanical type to the mental. Any one of these specific modes of motion can be converted into another under the proper material-historical conditions. And there are undoubtedly important aspects of material motion which remain to be discovered.

A similar diversity can be discerned in the views on the nature of matter and its structure brought forward at successive stages of materialist thought. These range from the simple conception of primary substance *(physis)* among the Greeks as composed of one or multiple elements through the Hobbesian conception of substance as extended body to the modern evolutionary concept of matter embracing unrestricted determinations of material existence from subatomic particles and galactic systems to living, feeling, thinking humans.

Passing from nature to society, we can note an equally wide variation in the historical outlooks, social standpoints and moral codes of the materialist schools. Although both the ancient and modern schools rested on a materialist conception of the world and man's place in it, the social orientation of the Epicureans, for example, stood at the opposite pole from that of Marxism. The Epicureans counseled submission to nature, withdrawal from worldly concerns and political strife, the practice of contemplation. Its dominant tone was passive, restrictive, pessimistic. As against this philosophy of resignation, dialectical materialism is aggressive toward nature, urging its progressive alteration for the sake of human welfare;

revolutionary in its intervention in social and political affairs; and places practical activity above theoretical contemplation. It has an energetic, expansive, optimistic and endlessly reconstructive outlook.

The striking differences between these two historical forms of materialism stem not only from the different levels of social and scientific development in which they originated and functioned but from the very different class forces they served. Epicureanism emerged in the transition from the Greek city-state to the Alexandrian and Roman Empires; it expressed the recoil of upper and middle-class elements from the disintegration of the old community life and their inability to find secure and stable places for themselves in the new cosmopolitan regimes. The Epicureans were suspended between two worlds: one dying, the other repellent to them. They had no creative function to play in either system.

Marxism, on the other hand, is the ideological instrument of the industrial working class which, while also caught in a declining social system, is itself the bearer and constructor of a new and higher order and is going forward to effect the transition with social confidence and theoretical understanding.

This particular contrast shows that, while materialism is the most correct and progressive of philosophies, it has not invariably been associated with the most progressive social strata, as some commentators assert. There is no simple, direct, one-to-one correspondence between world views and social dynamics. Once in existence, the ideas of materialism could be adapted to the needs of various social forces at specific stages of their careers. Hobbes, the monarchist, was a materialist during the same period of English revolution in the 17th Century that plebeian leaders of the Levellers like Overton also projected materialist ideas. These represented two contemporary but opposing social varieties of the same philosophical position, one aristocratic, the other democratic in affiliation.

All the materialist schools have developed lopsidedly. At one end the Milesians were the first to define the concept of nature—but they did not touch upon the problems of knowledge. At the other end the founders of Marxism probed the dynamics of social evolution to their ultimate source but were not able to do as much with the laws of nature. Engels had to leave unfinished his brilliant beginnings in the *Dialectics of Nature.*

What one school failed to deal with adequately, its successor took up and even overdeveloped. The one-sidedness of each stage had to be corrected by the further advances of scientific and philosophical thought, leading in the end to the present many-sided conception.

Despite their unavoidable inadequacies, each of the great schools brought forth new aspects of materialist thought in its own way and at its own time. Each contributed essential elements to the creation of the whole by deepening the understanding of nature, society, the human mind and their interrelations, thus producing progressively more penetrating degrees of insight into reality.

Not the least of these insights was the recognition that materialism is basically incompatible with idealism. The clear-cut opposition between these two standpoints set forth in such categorical terms at the beginning of this chapter was not evident at the birth of philosophy. This understanding too is an historical achievement, the upshot of 2,500 years of social and scientific investigation and of internal conflicts in the domain of philosophy itself. Even today the necessity for maintaining this opposition is denied by muddle-heads who have an interest, often unconscious, in perpetuating confusion about their real relations. To do this is to erase the progressive results of centuries of intellectual labor and regress to the infancy of philosophy.

The differences between the materialist and idealist standpoints and methods were well known and often discussed by the later Greek thinkers. But the respective positions of the opposing camps had yet to be worked out in full detail. The substantial differences between them were sometimes submerged and obscured in the common offensive of the entire enterprise of critical and rational thought aganst old religious ideas and customary institutions.

Still more important was the fact that materialism required the coexistence, conflict and contributions of its idealist antagonist in order to elicit its own full potential and acquire a comprehensive application. Idealism did more than simply prod materialism onward by criticism from the outside. The enduring insights which its exponents from Socrates to Hegel obtained into this or that sector of reality were later incorporated into the structure of materialism.

No single school has monopolized the discovery of

new ideas in the evolution of philosophy, especially in its most creative periods. Although the Greek materialists saw the essential reality of the objective world more correctly than the idealists, their views were defective in other respects. On the other hand, almost every idealist school from the Eleatics to the Skeptics and Stoics added something new and valuable to the understanding of reality, despite their errors on fundamental issues.

On the whole the idealists contributed far more to the theory of knowledge than to the theory of nature. But even in this latter field they offered notable innovations. While the Atomists first conceived that nature consisted of small particles moving in a void whose combinations and recombinations made up the passing show of events, the Pythagoreans first pictured nature as composed of mathematical relations and measurable quantities. Both views were valid and valuable. But in ancient society they remained distinct from each other and were pushed to their limits by separate trends of thought.

It was not until the 17th Century, when the development of mechanics coincided with the revival of atomism through Galileo and Gassendi, that these two hitherto antagonistic approaches to natural phenomena were brought together in a novel synthesis under new historical conditions. Their mutual fructification finally flowered into Dalton's atomic hypothesis which revolutionized the foundations of chemistry.

A similar union of previously unconnected and opposing lines of thought took place in the development of 19th Century European philosophy when the dialectical logic formulated and systematized by the arch-idealist Hegel was detached from its idealist cocoon and integrated into materialism by the originators of Marxism.

The opposition between idealism and materialism adumbrated among the Greeks was much more forcibly manifested when materialism came forward again with the rise of bourgeois society and acquired a sharp stamp with the struggles against medievalism and the advance of the sciences from the 16th to the 19th Centuries. This is demonstrated by the fact that materialism was then given a durable name of its own which unmistakably distinguished it from all rivals. The word materialism first gained currency in the epoch of Robert Boyle, the illustrious English physicist and chemist, who mentions "materialists" along with "naturalists" in his essay written in 1674 called *The Excellence and Grounds of the Mechanical Hypothesis.* Although Boyle was a pious Protestant, he gave an impetus to scientific materialism through his exposition of the mechanical conception of nature.

The term was taken up by the German philosopher Leibnitz in his *Reply to the Thoughts of (Pierre) Bayle,* the French skeptic, written in 1702. Leibnitz, who was himself an outstanding idealist, consciously counterposed idealism to materialism as the main contenders in philosophy. He traced the opposition between the mechanical type of thought in natural science and his own all the way back to the Greeks and saw it foreshadowed in the

contending doctrines of Epicurus, the materialist, and Plato, the idealist.

The opposition was made still sharper by Bishop
Berkeley from the side of idealism and then by Kant,
who occupied an in-between position. It was finally
nailed down by the materialist criticism of the idealists
conducted by Diderot, D'Holbach and their colleagues
in the latter half of the 18th Century, continuing
with Feuerbach in Germany, and concluding with
the Marxists of the next century.

In the course of these chapters we shall follow the
movement of philosophy in more specific detail and
see precisely how and why materialism and idealism, implicitly opposed from their birth, were hatched
from the shell of philosophy amidst the class struggles
of Greece, acquired their definite traits, came to grips
with each other for the first time and strove for supremacy. Now, in our own time, they stand arrayed
against each other in a mortal combat for complete
possession of the provinces of rational thought and
scientific knowledge.

[handwritten marginalia: "opposite", "spirit", "matter (result of; collective actions of human beings)", "idealism individual actions of human beings"]

II. The Real Basis of Materialism

A CONSISTENT MATERIALISM cannot proceed from principles which are presumably validated by appeal to abstract reason, intuition, self-evidence or some other subjective or purely theoretical source. Idealisms may do this. But the materialist philosophy has to be based upon evidence taken from objective material sources and verified by demonstration in practice. The real foundations and the causal origins of materialism can only be located in the material conditions of human life based on the sequence of social stages which have determined the various forms and changing content of thought.

The material basis, the historical source, the raw materials for the materialist outlook are lodged primarily in the actions, and the results of the collective actions, of human beings. These comprise both their past actions as registered in history and their

17

present ones; what they have had to do since humanity parted from the rest of the anthropoids and what men do every day here and now. Materialism derives its life, its meaning, its power, its validity from its inseparable connections with the habitual, inescapable, million-times-repeated practices of every member of the human race.

Idealists, echoing the religious dogma of St. John, claim that: "In the Beginning was the Word." This is fundamentally false. The Word, the concept, the formulated principle, the critical understanding, and philosophy, including the philosophy of materialism, all come after the Deed. Intellectual activities and ideological products take second place in life and in history to the practical actions of mankind. They are, in fact, an outgrowth of them.

The most important human activities are those centered around securing the means of existence. In their persistent round of efforts to get food, clothing, shelter and other basic necessities of life men run up against stubborn, resistant material realities with which they have to cope and to which they have to conform in order to survive and thrive.

Humans, however, do not simply submit to these external forces of their environment; they strive to turn its constituent elements to their advantage by gathering, using, altering and producing them. This conscious collective attack upon nature through the activities of labor is peculiar to the human species. In the struggle for life nature acts upon the social group which in turn pits itself against nature and proceeds to transform it for its own purposes.

However sharply people may feel the friction between themselves and other things in particular instances, humanity in its infancy is unaware of any basic opposition between the environment and itself. On the contrary, the essential organic unity between themselves and the rest of reality is taken for granted as an unconscious assumption of practical life.

It requires a highly civilized and scientifically sophisticated intelligence to distinguish mankind, as a separate entity, from everything else that exists and counterpose humanity to nature clearly and constantly. Primitive peoples have not yet severed the umbilical cord binding them to Mother Nature. They view themselves as all of a piece with animals, plants and even physical events, putting these other parts and phenomena of nature on the same footing as themselves.

This kind of a materialist attitude is spontaneous, naive, almost instinctive. It is ages removed from any generalized conception of materialism. It exists below the threshold of consciousness. Between this most primitive attitude to nature, arising from everyday practice, to an explicit materialistic formulation of man's position in the universe there had to be a path of development extending over hundreds of thousands of years.

Nevertheless, these incessantly renewed and tested ties with the external world are the starting point and remain the actual foundation of any materialist outlook. It is in and through the practical activities emanating from the social struggle for survival that the real relations between man and nature have been bit by bit revealed.

All of humanity, from the first tool-using primates to ourselves, have acted upon such a "natural" belief in the independent existence and real priority of the external world. This is the persistent materialism of mankind. Hume, the English philosopher of the 18th Century, took note of this common-sense belief as follows: "It seems evident that men are carried by a natural instinct or prepossession to repose faith in their senses; and that, without any reasoning, or even almost before the use of reason, we always suppose an external universe, which depends not on our perceptions, but would exist though we and every sensible creature were absent or annihilated." *

*Hume's own reasoning led him to the skeptical conclusion that such belief in the independent and prior existence of an external world could not be rationally justified. He could find no evidence in his own or others' experience to substantiate the assertion. At the same time he felt obliged to admit that not only the rest of humanity but himself, the reasonable skeptic, as well had to act in everyday affairs as through this belief were true.

This was a humiliating and awkward position for Hume to be in, and it was not in fact a tenable one, either in theory or in practice. However, his exposure of the need for providing sufficient reasons for our faith in the external world prodded philosophical through forward.

Dr. Johnson, Hume's contemporary, ridiculed the results of this reasoning and sought to refute Berkeley's denial and Hume's doubts about the materiality of the external world by kicking a stone. This gesture was an effective denial of Hume's skepticism in practice. But Hume himself had acknowledged that in practice he had to feel and act like everyone else. What he demanded was logical grounds and direct evidence in experience for validating the common-sense belief in the substantiality of material things. Hume's arguments had to be met and countered on the higher level of philosophical theory. That was what Kant, among others, tried to do. But it was not until the advent of dialectical materialism that complete and correct materialist answers to Hume's skeptical criticisms were given.

It is a matter of fact that every waking minute of our lives every one of us acts upon the premise that there is the external world existing independently of us and exerting its influences upon us. Ordinary activity, work, communication could not go on without assuming this truth. Nothing is so continually and thoroughly tested in *practice*, the supreme court of truth, as the belief in the real existence of this real world around us. This ever-renewed activity of mankind provides the most direct testimony and the most compelling evidence of the validity of the materialist view of the world and our relation to it. This fact of practice likewise provides the ultimate refutation of all kinds of agnosticism, skepticism and idealism regarding the independent existence of nature and our ability to know it.

Our conviction of the material nature of reality is vindicated not simply by man's contacts with an external, independent, recalcitrant nature standing ever against him, like an immovable obstacle. Mankind is not passively bound to the natural environment and dragged along with it like an unresisting captive in chains. Mankind is above all an active and re-active force that comes to grips with nature and compels it to serve its needs.

The most convincing evidence of the real and necessary existence of the material world is given by mankind's own assimilation and alteration of natural substances. The physiological processes by which we convert external matter into our own body, our own life, our own sensation and even thought provides daily proof of the truth of materialism. Through the acts of breathing, eating and drinking we continually transform the elements of nature into our own human substance. Our utter dependence upon material things shows up when the lack of oxygen, food and drink produces asphyxiation, starvation and thirst, and in the advent of disease and even death when minerals, vitamins and other vital ingredients are not supplied to the organism.

Science has charted the main steps in the circulation of the energy required by life, demonstrating that all vital processes are bound up with the conversion of energy from one form and source to another in the ceaseless interactions of nature. With minor exceptions all the energy used by life originates in the sun and comes to the earth as radiation. It is then captured by plants and turned into chemical energy. From plants the energy is transmitted to other organisms, including the animals that eat plants and one another. From these two sources the energy becomes part of human beings and their diverse functions. At every step of this energy-cycle one form of matter is used up and converted into another until it ceases to be available for further use by living creatures. These nevertheless continue to be dependent upon new energy received from the sun.

Mankind is not only physically dependent upon nature; he is both physically and socially dependent upon his fellow human beings. Humans cannot be propagated except through the coitus of persons belonging to materially different sexes. The infant cannot obtain nurture except through an adult. At all times the individual is indissolubly associated with the other members of our species.

He has a dual relation with them. His associates are like him, act with him, aid him. Through them and with them he gets the necessary means of life. At the same time they differ from him, are separate from him, opposed to him. They have bodies, wills, minds of their own. These are the material realities that infants have to learn about and reckon with.

All these physical relations and social interactions testify to the independent reality of nature and society and to the material nature of the individual's connections with them.

III. Magic and Religion

THE PHYSICAL TIES BETWEEN mankind and nature are the basic support of materialism; the procreative functions which constitute the genetic connections of men are part of these.

But materialism has a second source of support in the productive relations which bind the members of society together in their joint dealings with the environment. Individual men do not face nature directly. Between nature and the individual stands the structure of society based upon the mode of producing the necessities of life. The forces and relations of production mediate between nature and men and determine the characteristics of their interplay at any given stage of historical development.

By acting upon nature and transforming its materials for the satisfaction of his needs, said Marx, man first forms and then transforms his own nature. But the way in which man acts upon nature, and

24

nature upon him depends upon what means of production he has. The Indians of Southern California, for example, remained food gatherers; they could not engage in agriculture largely because of the aridity of the area. Today this same land through aqueducts and irrigation facilities has become one of the world's richest agricultural regions.

The effectiveness and extent of man's activities, including his mental activity, hinge upon the level of his powers of material production. These powers have multiplied as society has improved its technology. The existing level and special traits of men's theorizing are determined by the character of their productive activities and the social and cultural institutions shaped by them. The prevailing picture that people have of nature and their connections with it is formed by the degree of the practical control of their social order over its operations. Stone Age tribes, who acquire their means of sustenance through gathering food and remain in the foraging, hunting or fishing stages of economy, have images of their surroundings corresponding to their extremely feeble capacities of production and simple social relations.

Thus the intellectual grasp of reality is a function of social control over reality. Where such control is minimal, the understanding is poorly developed and highly distorted. Primitive peoples satisfy their needs, like anyone else, in prosaic materialistic ways. But the reflections in their minds of the world around them, their conceptions of the features and creatures within it, themselves included, take on fantastic shapes. The low level of their capacities for material production becomes a breeding ground for non-materialist views of reality.

The consciousness of primitive peoples does not penetrate their environment deeply or understand its relations very accurately. The savage who lives in such close proximity to the wilderness knows less on the whole about the true character of its operations, and his own connections with them, than the civilized man.

Two very different types of activities and ideas coexist in the savage life and mentality. Solidly connecting them with reality are certain technical skills based upon genuine knowledge of the properties and processes of the world around them. These have been acquired from the success of their collective practical efforts in securing the necessities of life. Savages can be keen-eyed food collectors, expert hunters and trappers, skilled fishermen, industrious and nimble craftsmen, successful gardeners. Without a social fund of practical know-how which works for them as they work, that is, produces real results every day which satisfy their wants, they could neither have survived in the struggle for existence nor raised themselves so far above animal life.

Primitive women have learned to distinguish edible plants from non-edible ones, and even to convert poisonous roots like manioc into food. They have to conserve and make fire and use it for diverse purposes. They must know how to build shelters and make clothing. Primitive hunters have to observe the habits of game, learn how to make devices to capture and slay animals, find out how to utilize their products and by-products. The raising of the simplest crops requires many kinds of information: the selection of soil and seeds, the right way to clear the garden, seasonal timing, protection against pests and marauders, etc.

These activities of production in foraging, hunting, fishing, gardening and crude craftsmanship are the seeds of science and the great grandparents of materialist philosophy.

However, the sector of nature which primitive men dominate is very small compared to the mysteries of the unknown and the uncontrollable pressing in on them from all sides. Along with the practical knowledge arising from their productive activities, which is true, rational and effective so far as it reaches, there emerges another kind of activities and ideas which is false, irrational and incapable of doing what it intends or pretends. This mass of rituals and grotesque conceptions growing out of the immense area of enigmatic and unmastered phenomena has been designated by the term "magic."

Magic takes up where man's effective control over nature gained by technology leaves off. Primitive people know that they have to plant seeds and cultivate the ground to get a harvest. At the same time they are aware of the limitations imposed upon their efforts. No matter how arduous the labors or great their skill, they may not capture enough game, be favored with a good crop or any at all. Pests, foraging animals, bad weather and many other natural factors which affect their vital needs for good or ill remain beyond community control. Yet the tribe desperately depends for its survival upon success in these enterprises.

Uncivilized peoples have no alternative for offsetting the deficiencies of their social economy except through the methods of magic. Magic is designed to satisfy demands and desires which social life has awakened but does not yet have the means to guarantee. The techniques of magic assume that other superior and supernatural powers exist who can influence the course of events for weal or woe and therefore have to be counteracted, neutralized or won over.

Imaginary powers are fabricated out of the creatures, natural elements and humans which impress themselves most powerfully upon the primitive imagination. They may be ancestors, elders or chiefs, animals or plants, mountains, rain, thunder, the moon or the sun. These actual or once-existing beings are invested with properties and powers which they do not actually possess or exercise. The savages have these abilities in a limited measure but they crave more of them. So they project their desires for the unobtained means of satisfaction into external objects and then hopefully contrive by magical means to get back what they have given.

"Magic rests on the principle that by creating the illusion that you control reality you can actually control it. It is an illusory technique complementary to the deficiencies of the real technique. Owing to the low level of production the human consciousness is as yet imperfectly aware of the objectivity of the external world, which accordingly it treats as though changeable at will, and so the preliminary rite is regarded as the cause of success in the real task; but at the same time, as a guide to action, the ideology of magic embodies the valuable truth that the external world can be changed by man's subjective attitude toward it."—*Studies in Ancient Greek Society* by George Thomson, Vol. I, pp. 38-39.

The savage mind views nature in its own social image, personifying its phenomena and humanizing its parts. Primitive peoples are so merged with, so submerged by their natural surroundings that they draw no sharp demarcations between themselves and the rest of their world, including its plant and animal life. They interpret their whole environment in accord with their own social relations and customary modes of activity. They endow nature, or project into its elements, the same type of kinship ties and the same powers of will, initiative and consciousness they possess.

Material objects like stones and trees or natural events like thunder and lightning are incorporated into their own outlook as kinfolk or as stranger-enemies, as bearers of good or evil. It is naively believed that these can think, speak or act like themselves or are produced by beings with motives and aims like their own.

Anything of importance in savage life can be drawn into the network of magic. The Maoris of New Zealand, for example, looked upon trees and mountains as beings like themselves with whom they had close kinship relations. The Fiji Islanders ask permission of coconut trees before they pluck their nuts. In a yearly ritual the Huron Indians married their nets or seines to two little girls to render themselves fortunate in catching fish.

If one of the Kookies is killed by a wild beast, the whole tribe takes vengeance upon the animal as they would upon a strange tribe. It is not essential that the very animal be slain so long as it is one of the same species. On the other hand, they believe that the whole of the animal's clan will take up the blood feud on behalf of any one of them against the Kookies. If a falling tree has killed a kinsman, they cut it up into fine splinters and scatter them to the winds.

This absorption of animals and plants into their totemic organization of social life with its personification of the forces of nature leads to a curious dialectical development. The uncritical and unconditional identification of the rest of the world with themselves which is at the core of the instinctive materialism of primitive peoples gives birth to that animistic outlook which is the starting point of the religious view of the universe. The principle of animism accounts for events through the agency of personalized natural powers which become supernatural. Animism is common to magic and religion; it later becomes extended through idealism into the field of philosophy.

In pre-civilized life the practices and beliefs of magic do not function apart from the practices based upon propositions of empirical knowledge. The two are matted together in a single outlook upon the surrounding world. Procreation and production, the twin material bases of group existence, are enveloped in the mystifications of magic. The primitive mind looks upon the making of an image of the creature to be hunted or the mimicking of the slaying of a tribal foe as no less potent and instrumental in ensuring the success of hunting and warfare than the physical acts of tipping and shooting the arrows or crashing a club over the enemy's skull. The magical rites play the same role as prayers, holy water and the blessing of the priests in later religious ceremonies.

Evidences of sympathetic magic have been traced back thirty thousand years or so to the creators of the paleolithic cave paintings found in France and Spain. These earliest artists almost exclusively painted or modelled game animals. Many of these meat providers are depicted as pregnant.

The mammoths, reindeer and other animals were not drawn for the aesthetic pleasure of the beholders but for the utilitarian purpose of ensuring magical possession of the wild beasts upon which their livelihoods depended. By drawing them with spears and arrows in their hides the hunter-artists aimed to insure the tribe that the hunt would not fail.

Before the Agricultural Revolution the collective control of savage men over the processes of nature, while sufficient to enable them to survive and progress, was extremely scanty. All the greater therefore was the place occupied by magical ways and means devised to overcome that weakness.

Under barbarism magic passes over gradually into the higher form of religion without changing its essential nature. Religion has a two-fold historical root. Like magic, it remains a cultural expression of man's lack of control over nature. Unlike magic, religion comes to reflect the growth of man's loss of control over the forces of his social life which is the ironic eventual outcome of food production.

Food production had anomalous consequences. On the one hand, it assured pastoral and agricultural peoples of an ample and expanding food supply for the first time. In its further development, however, it made possible a social division of labor and a growth of craftsmanship and trade which led to the accumulation of surpluses of wealth in the most favored communities. These provided an economic pedestal for the rise of non-productive ruling groups.

As barbarism advanced and passed over into civilization, the previously cohesive tribes began to be differentiated into chieftains, rulers, priesthoods and nobles who took command of the processes of production and exacted tribute from the actual producers. These divisions in society had their reflections in a new type of social consciousness that endowed everything and everyone with a double constitution and a divided existence. For example, an anima, spirit, soul was supposed to inhabit the body, though distinct from it and able to leave it during dreams, sneezing, death and other incidents. The personified powers of nature and dead ancestors became transformed into ghosts, goblins, genii, local spirits, trolls, elves, pixies, leprechauns, fairies, witches, demons, devils and gods.

The great world religions like Judaism, Christianity, Buddhism, Mohammedanism took over the crude magical ideas born of primitive impotence and ignorance and refined them into the familiar oppositions of God and man, soul and body, spirit and matter, just as their religious ceremonies imitate the rituals and incantations of the witch-doctor and his tribesmen. God, soul and spirit were exalted as all-powerful and immortal, of quite different stuff from the perishable body, degraded matter and sinful mankind. Thus religion, and in its wake, idealist philosophy, perpetuated the division in the nature of being fostered by the first class formations and initiated by the primitive notion of the manikin-soul inside man as well as in many other creatures and objects.

The Lord's Prayer which is taught to children at home, in church and at school shows how the core of magic persists in the Christianity of today. This incantation is a composite of elements gathered along the way from primitive magic to civilized religion. It goes back, according to scholars, to Sumerian cults.

Its content, purpose and tone differs in detail but not in substance from the utterances in the mumbo-jumbos of the savages. The magician, witch-doctor and shaman are lineal ancestors of the priest, pastor and rabbi.

Let us interpret its phrases to see how children are tutored in superstition. The humble petitioner in need first addresses "Our Father"—a heavenly edition of the patriarch and ruler in class society. This despot is then elevated far above mortals to divine dimensions: "Who art in Heaven." He receives the reverence due to superior authority: "Hallowed be Thy name." The petitioner asks that his wishes be fulfilled: "Thy Kingdom come; Thy Will be done." Not later but here and now: "On earth as it is in Heaven."

As the savage demands a good harvest and a fine catch from his magical provider, so the civilized "savage" begs: "Give us this day our daily bread."

He asks to be purified of taboos violated: "And forgive us our trespasses." This is supplemented by the moralizing influence of Christian culture: "As we forgive those of others." This is crowned by the admission of weakness, humility, fear, awe, submission to the dominant superhuman power: "For Thine is the power and glory forever." The parting injunction of "Amen" signifies: so be it, don't fail us.

The endurance of magic can also be seen in such customs as sending flowers to funerals and placing wreaths on graves. This rite comes down from the primitive belief in another existence after death; the departed soul needs the same things as in earthly life. Savages and barbarians buried food, utensils and weapons as well as household slaves, mates and warriors with the remains of dead notables. These burial customs have today dwindled down to the token placement of a few flowers on the grave. Whatever reasons may be offered for retaining the ritual, which even many materialists and atheists continue to practice, it harks back to conceptions of life and death belonging to the infancy of mankind.

The minds of pre-civilized peoples are dominated by magical and religious views of the world. These are the modes of representing reality characteristic of savagery and barbarism. Peoples living in pre-civilized conditions have neither the material means nor the cultural needs to ascend to the level of philosophical generalizations. They represent their relations with the rest of the world and with one another in magical and religious forms.

Despite the slowly growing store of positive

knowledge at their command, which in time paves the way for the first schools of philosophy and the first branches of science, the earlier ages of social evolution from the dawn of man to the end of barbarism are as barren of philosophy as they are of alphabetic writing, coinage, and the use of machinery. These are cultural creations of a higher grade of social activity. Philosophy as a special type of theorizing about the conditions of human life, and materialism as a special type of philosophical reasoning, belong historically to commercial centers based upon a well-developed division of social labor.

IV. The Road to Philosophy

THERE ARE FEW PROBLEMS IN the history of culture more engrossing and important than the origins of philosophy. One obligation of a philosopher, and a good test of his method, is to explain how his particular branch of thought came into existence.

This question can be answered only if it is approached along the avenue of social evolution—and revolution. We have first to stress the negative point that the ideological forms peculiar to philosophy did not exist among savages or barbarians. Its special techniques of thought did not come to life in a sleepy backwoods community or among nomads in a desert. Philosophy failed to make an appearance even in the agricultural kingdoms of Mesopotamia and Egypt. These facts signify that none of these peoples possessed all the material and cultural prerequisites for producing and practising this mode of thought.

36

Philosophy was born in the commercial centers of Aegean civilization in the 6th Century B.C. It was the cultural achievement of a bustling maritime city life. The first recorded school of philosophy was located in Miletus, one of the cities settled by Ionian Greeks on the coast of Asia Minor opposite the Greek mainland.

Thus, at the outset, we are confronted by a dual historical problem. First, why didn't philosophy emerge before the 6th Century B.C.? Second, why did philosophy (and science) originate among the Greeks of Ionia, and why did materialism take shape around that particular time and place?

The answer to the first part of this problem is to be found in the historical succession of ideologies from magic through religion to philosophy which grew out of and reflected the development of society from savagery through barbarism to civilization. The discrimination of magical rites and beliefs and of religious superstitions and myths from genuine empirical knowledge of the world, and their conscious counterposition to one another, is essentially the product of a high urban culture. Certain backward peoples have not attained it to this very day.

Even after they have crossed over to civilization, the most advanced peoples have required a protracted social-economic development before they could reach the point of casting off magic and religion and moving intellectually beyond them. A prodigious number of historical changes, improvements in technology, transformations of social structures and definitions of categories of thought had to be realized before the vanguard of humanity could shake off primeval outlooks and arrive at the method of philosophical reasoning.

These changes go all the way back to the introduction of agriculture around 8-10,000 B.C. Some of the other principal landmarks along the way to philosophy were the emergence of city life around 4000 B.C. the discovery of iron-smelting and the spread of iron for tool-making about 1100 B.C., and the creation of the alphabet and the diffusion of literacy several centuries later.

The Agricultural Revolution gave mankind control over its food supply for the first time; stimulated the growth of religion; and brought into being the first elements of knowledge required for philosophy and science. There is a close connection between agriculture, religion and the rudiments of science. Food gatherers and hunters do not need to mark the passage of time except in the broadest ways and had only the dimmest notions of its periodic regularities. The seasonal requirements of farming occupations with their regular and regulated round of production make the study of the flow of time an economic necessity and a social function for the first time. Men were forced to pay attention to certain regularities in the movement of the seasons and the heavenly bodies because their sustenance depended upon them. The need to devise ways and means of measuring time led to the invention of calendars and the first astronomical discoveries. That is why priesthoods became the creators and custodians of primitive science.

This sequence of development can be observed not only among the civilizations situated in the irrigated river valleys of Mesopotamia and Egypt but also in the valleys of Central America and on the plateaus of the Andes and Mexico where the highest levels of Indian culture in the Western hemisphere were attained. Let us take the Aztecs as a case in point. Their tribal religion, with collective rites embracing the entire people, was rooted in the cultivation of maize. Their religious ceremonies revolved around the calendar devised by the priesthood. These medicine men, as custodians of this knowledge, were the supervisors of the magical ceremonies. They supplicated natural elements like the rain and the mountains which had been converted into personalized social powers to whom they offered presents and made human sacrifices. All these rituals were bound up with the agricultural operations upon which the lives of the Aztecs depended. Their economy, their religion, their proto-science were all fused together.

These American Indians proceeded up to the borderline between barbarism and civilization. They had a folk religion but no philosophy; calendars and the beginnings of empirical astronomy but no theoretical science; they had bronze but no iron; picture writing but no alphabet.

Many other fundamental historical achievements were necessary before philosophy and natural science could be born. One was the establishment of city life containing concentrated populations with diverse classes carrying on specialized functions: priests, kings, nobles, officials, merchants, metal workers and other

craftsmen. The conquests of several thousand years
of city culture enabled mankind to separate itself,
in thought as well as in material production, from
total immersion in nature and domination by it.

The crowning touch was given to technology in
ancient times by the spread of iron. All the major
hand tools had been perfected by the Iron Age. This
cheap metal enabled peasants to have more efficient
agricultural implements: sickles, hoes, ploughshares,
axes, shears, shovels. Metalworkers, carpenters, shoe-
makers, masons and a host of other artisans en-
hanced their productivity with iron tools. The combination of city culture and iron tools raised engineering to a new level. Engineers with iron tools cut a
tunnel one-third of a mile long through a mountain
to bring water to Samos before 500 B.C. This admirable feat of construction deserves special mention
because Samos was one of the Ionian Greek cities
where philosophy had its birth.

The widespread use of iron brought about a basic
change in the relations between industry and agriculture. "The greatly increased productivity of agriculture yielded a surplus which could support a large
number of specialized craftsmen. The product of the
craftsman became generally available instead of being
the monopoly of the wealthy. In particular the craftsman provided for the farmer those same tools with
which the latter increased the productivity of his work.
And thus, for the first time, there arose a balanced
relationship between industry and agriculture, instead
of the former one-sided relationship by which agriculture provided the food for the craftsman, but the

craftsman's product went only to the select few," points out S. Lilley, *Men, Machines and History* (p. 21).

Finally, the invention of the alphabet by the Phoenicians, which the Greeks took over around the late 8th Century B.C., broke down the monopoly of learning vested in the priests and scribes by making it possible for large numbers of people to read and write. In addition to diffusing knowledge more widely, the new literacy promoted the development of abstract thought, permitted speech and thought to become objects of special study, and thus paved the way for the science of grammar and logic in which the Greeks excelled.

All the conditions of social practice which could render magic and religion obsolete and give rise to a superior mode of reasoning and theoretical outlook were not gathered together at one time and in one place until the 6th Century B.C. Philosophy, materialism and the method of science associated with them are original creations of the Greeks. Their culture appears to us as the dawn of our modern era, the ancient source of our own civilization. Retrospectively, it was the continuation and culmination of the Agricultural, Urban and Metallic revolutions which lifted mankind out of the Stone Age, dispelled the mists of magic from nature, and the mystifications of mythology from generalized thought.

Behind the Greeks stood the achievements of the Cretans and Myceneans, the Phoenicians and the Hittites, the Sumerians, Babylonians, Egyptians and others. Greek philosophy was the ripe fruitage of the efforts and knowledge of all these Middle Eastern

and Mediterranean peoples. The Greeks took the
rudiments of mathematics and astronomy from the
Babylonians and Egyptians, medicine from the
Mesopotamians and Egyptians, and writing from
the Phoenicians. To the materials derived from these
rich and varied cultures the Greeks added their own
special contributions and fashioned a uniquely new
type of thought and world outlook.

This new type of thought did not sweep away the
more archaic outlooks when it appeared. Quite the
contrary. The preponderant influence among the Greek
people in all stations of life remained with the old
forms. Every civilized society has been composed
of elements stemming from different stages of material and cultural evolution. Such interpenetrations of
the old with the new were present throughout classical Greek history. Just as the Greeks continued to use
stone and bronze implements along with iron ones,
so magic and religion were amalgamated in their
cultural life with the earliest sprouts of the new
philosophical and scientific thought.

The ideas and usages of primitive magic and religious superstition not only preceded and surrounded
philosophy; they even permeated it to some extent
and eventually triumphed over rationalism in the
ancient world. The old and the new were sometimes
fused together in the head of the same thinker or the
doctrines of the same school. Among the Pythagoreans, for example, taboos against meat-eating, hero-
worship, number-mysticism were woven together with
ethics, science and philosophy into a single cult; the
poem in which Parmenides expounded his philosophy

was patterned upon the hymns recited by the votaries of the Mysteries; and even the materialistic Epicureans acquired certain features of a religious association.

From the peasant in the countryside to the cosmopolitan aristocrat, the Greeks carried along a heavy load of practices and beliefs from their barbarous past. Most of the religious calendar of the Greek cities was, like that of the Aztecs, bound up with the most important operations of the agricultural cycle.

The three greatest festivals of Athens coincided with the dates fixed for ploughing, vine-dressing and harvest. These celebrations were filled with ancient rites of a purely magical character. At the *Thesmophoria,* held in honor of the Mother-Goddess Demeter, married women, after purifying themselves by appropriate ceremonies for nine days, thrust pigs, branches of pine, images of corn, and even, in some places, human genital organs into the ground to promote its fertility. During the three-day springtime festival of the *Anthesteria,* celebrated by every Ionian community, the thresholds were sprinkled with peas to ward off the evil spirits and souls of the dead that were thought to march through the place.

Hesiod lists lucky and unlucky days of the month. Contact with the dead and with tombs was supposed to contaminate people and provoke the vengeance of evil spirits unless certain purifying precautions were taken. A child whose parents were dead was not permitted to perform many acts.

The Greeks practiced black magic and witchcraft in which images of prospective victims were tortured and buried to deal harm to them. They relied upon the charms and spells of sorcerers to drive demons out of sick people. They were accustomed to offer both animal and human scapegoats to expel evil from their communities and made sacrifices to expiate guilts and propitiate offended supernatural forces.

There was hardly a belief or ceremony of magic known to tribal life that did not remain alive in some part of Greece. The two are so thoroughly intermixed that it would be impossible to sift out the magical components from the rest of the religious practices of the Greeks. These were rooted in the cult of heroic dead ancestors nurtured by the military notables of their barbaric age. Greek religion was a conglomerate of rites and beliefs drawn from the cults of the Cretans, the patriarchal tribes of the Achaean invaders and the Myceneans. Zeus, for example, originally belonged to a Minoan band of demons for whom he danced and practiced rites of fertilizing magic.

The Homeric poets elevated these nature and ancestral gods to the heights of Mount Olympus, invested them with humanized features, and hierarchized them on the model of the society of conquering chieftains and royal buccaneers for whom they were the minstrels. There were all sorts of gods in addition to the pantheon: local, family and clan gods, nature gods, wood-nymphs and river deities, goddesses of justice, etc. The savage origin of these deities stands out sharply in such half-bestial figures as the goat-god Pan, a vestige of primitive totemism who survives to the present day in the cloven hooves and tail of the Christian devil.

The Greeks consulted oracles at sacred places such

as the temple of Zeus at Dodona, the temples of Apollo near Miletus and at Delphi. Priesthoods pretended to divine the past and future by reading whispering leaves, smoke signals or animal entrails. The Greeks welcomed and adapted to their own needs foreign cults and deities as readily as they borrowed other ideas and customs. They took the Eleusinian Mysteries from Memphis and Phoenicia, the Orphic mysteries from Egypt, and the cult of Mithraism from Persia and celebrated their rites in the sanctuaries of temples.

The wonder is that philosophy should have been able to break through such a thick crust of time-honored superstition. Indeed, some scholars have denied that the divisions between the tribal conceptions, religious conceptions and the pre-Socratic philosophy of the Greeks are so sharp and deep as is usually supposed. They view them as affinities rather than opposites. (See appendix.)

The thought of all the Greek thinkers, even the most materialist, contained features taken from the most diverse sources and stages of ideological development. Thomson claims that Thales and Anaximander belonged to families of king-priests. It would be unhistorical to expect that any living cultural phenomenon, especially in its formative period, would be wholly free of contradictory elements.

Greek philosophy never shouldered Greek mythology and religion completely aside and secured supremacy for itself. They coexisted as competitors which to a certain extent had to come to terms with each other. The Greek mind and imagination did not

function in airtight compartments. The very mythology which had been set aside to make room for
natural philosophy was at the same time indispensable for Greek art: its literature, drama, sculpture,
music, festivals, etc. Philosophy could not avoid the
impress of mythology in such a cultural environment.
On the other hand, philosophy stamped its mark upon
the drama even when the playwrights used mythological themes.

One significant respect in which philosophy diverged
from its forerunners was in its birth process. Magic
and religion are collective productions of tribal origin carried over into urban life. The chief personages
connected with these ideologies are not historical but
mythical, or at least the mythical supersedes the social reality.

Philosophy, on the other hand, is the work of distinctive individuals. From the beginning philosophy
is linked with men who are real historical personalities, not imaginary figures like the heroes of folk tales
and the gods and saviors of the cults. The individualism and realism which mark off philosophical speculation from the more archaic outlooks are not
accidental but inherent traits of its ideology. They
arise from the specific historical circumstances of its
formation in a social structure of a higher type than
the old tribal and kinship relations, one in which individual ownership and its standards had begun to
flourish.

Let us now see how this new kind of civilization
came into existence.

DID EARLY GREEK PHILOSOPHY make a definitive break with all preceding views— or was it largely a continuation, in a more rationalized guise, of ancestral methods and ideas? This issue has been debated for almost half a century by English classical scholars and is still unsettled.

The champions of the contending views are Burnet and Cornford. Burnet, the author of *Early Greek Philosophy,* maintained that the Milesian contribution to thought was unique, original, qualitatively different from anything produced by the Babylonians, Egyptians, Indians, or their own predecessors in Greece. "A new thing came into the world with the early Ionian thinkers . . ."

On the other side, Cornford declared that, except in medicine, the Greeks before Aristotle were not scientific because they did not resort to experiment to test and check their speculations. The philosophers from Thales to Epicurus presented rationalized versions of ancient ideas inherited from Hesiod and the mythical cosmogonies of Babylon which in turn were rooted in the original totemic structures of savage tribes. He especially defined pre-Socratic philosophy as a more civilized and sophisticated remodelling of the tribal myths about the world, differing in form but not in essential content from the most primitive conceptions.

Which is correct? Did the Greek philosophers bring

forth something genuinely new in the domain of thought or did they do no more than transform the materials of primitive ideology handed down to them?

To the question posed in this way, it is necessary to agree with Burnet that the natural philosophers of Ionia were authentic innovators who broke away from traditional modes of thought and created an original method of conceiving the world and explaining man's position within it. They rejected supernaturalism of the mythical and religious varieties and sought to interpret the origins, development and features of the world by natural means and agencies. This was a revolutionary overturn of past methods.

The main movement of human thought has been from magic through religion to philosophy. Each of these represents a higher stage, no matter how much obsolete stuff is carried over from one stage to the next. If religion is a bridge from magic to philosophy, the latter rests on different foundations and lies on opposite grounds from the first two. This sequence of ideological development, blurred over in Cornford, is brought out, though one-sidedly, by Burnet.

However, this does not end the matter. The Greek thinkers did not step out of a void. In taking their gigantic step forward, they had to make use of materials handed down from the past—and it took considerable time and intellectual labor for them to get rid of the old junk. They never succeeded in eliminating all of it from their minds.

Cornford performed a great service for the understanding of Greek thought by uncovering the extremely primitive background out of which the pre-

Socratics emerged and which conditioned, though it did not fundamentally determine, their ideological outlook. He showed how the intellectual processes which bore their fruit in Miletus had begun centuries earlier and could be traced back to the rationalizing of the old myths and gods by the poets Homer and Hesiod. He also pointed out that the philosopher as a special type developed out of the wisemen of ancient Greece; in turn the wisemen, the prophet and poet were all descended from the shaman who was the supposedly inspired intermediary between his tribesmen and the supernatural.

Many of the earlier philosophers retained or combined one or several features of these functions. Empedocles was a poet and wiseman; the more prosaic Socrates was both wiseman and inspired prophet. Considerable mythical material remained embedded in the new philosophies. Heraclitus appealed to Justice as the regulator of physical processes; Empedocles has Eros-Love in his cosmology; and Plato turned to the inspired prophetess Diotima in his cosmological speculations. The traditions of the priestly cult persisted not only among the idealistic Pythagoreans but among the materialist Epicureans.

But these remnants of the past carried over to one degree or another were not so decisive or important as the new ideas and methods projected by the philosophers, and particularly the materialist-minded. They hatched something radically new. While Cornford shows the shell still clinging to the chick, he fails to give due weight to the distinctively new features and functions of the chick itself.

The philosophic mode of explaining the world was not a simple extension of the old under a new guise; it was a qualitatively different growth, arising out of a new set of historical conditions. The conclusions of the naturalists were much more than rationalized reproductions or reaffirmations of cosmological myths. At least so far as the materialists were concerned, they were revolutionary negations and rejections of them. Whatever old materials were reabsorbed were refashioned into something radically new in constitution and different in principle.

What is most significant about the early Greek savants is not their affiliations with the past but their departure from it. They did not merely grow out of the previous phases; they outgrew them and went beyond them. New conditions, forces, and discoveries exploded the former mythical concepts and gave birth to a new type of thought as a result. What is most important in their thinking is not where they travelled in the old ruts but where they diverged from them and came out on a new highway.

The basic differences between the mythologists and the materialists can be discerned by the comparison and analysis of their ideas. But the strongest proof of their difference can be judged from their consequences. "By their fruits shall ye know them." The later products of the early naturalists best testify to the new roots and different soil out of which they grew.

The idealist schools absorbed far more from the religious and mythological traditions than the materialists. Essentially they do represent a continuation of the older modes of thought in the new philosophical categories and techniques. In their case Cornford stands on firm ground. But he goes astray when he dismisses all the pre-Socratic schools, materialist and idealist alike, as non-scientific.

His main negative reason for doing so is that these early Greeks did not include experimentation in their methods. However, they did combine acute observation of natural processes with rational analysis based upon materialist premises. This was enough to give their procedures and conclusions a scientific character and foundation.

Experiment as a regular practice and a deliberated test of hypotheses is a necessary step in any well-rounded scientific method. But it is the product of a higher stage of scientific development and is not absolutely indispensable for scientific investigation. The observatory precedes the laboratory. Astronomy, one of the first and most advanced sciences, does not depend on experiment. Neither does political economy among the social sciences. Cornford's attempt to nullify the genuinely scientific direction of early Greek materialism by its absence of experiment does not hold water.

Cornford does not appreciate the novelty of Greek philosophy at its true value, slurs over the discontinuity between ancient mythology and the naturalist cosmologies, and effaces the vital differences between the materialist and idealist trends.

Burnet commits the opposite error, though a lesser one. He fails to give due weight to the elements of continuity in Greek thought transmitted from the older outlooks to the new.

By recognizing their respective limitations, it is possible to pass beyond the one-sidedness of their positions and arrive at a more rounded estimate of the pre-Socratics.

V. The Revolution
in Aegean Civilization

THE REVOLUTION IN HUMAN knowledge from which philosophy issued is bound up with that period in ancient history when the most advanced sectors of humanity passed from the Bronze Age over to the Iron Age and slavery developed from its patriarchal beginnings to a higher form based upon a more extensive division of social labor and an unprecedented expansion of trade. It was the ultimate product of a series of revolutionary changes in the lives of the peoples of the Eastern Mediterranean and the Middle East.

The nature and scope of these changes can best be grasped by contrasting some principal features of the two historical stages. The technology of the Bronze Age was rigidly restricted by the scarcity and expensiveness of that major metal which limited its use to weapons of war and articles of luxury. Bronze was an aristocratic material confined to the needs of the wealthy and placed beyond the reach of ordinary craftsmen and cultivators.

Once the processes of smelting the ore were mastered, iron was far more plentiful, cheap, and easily workable. With its introduction the use of metal spread for the first time through all strata of ancient society. This democratic material provided more efficient tools for the craftsman, stronger parts for the shipbuilder, better implements for the farmers and gave a powerful impetus to the productive forces in industry and agriculture.

On its own level this was a period of unprecedented technological innovation and advance. The immense enlargement in the body of workers accustomed to using metal tools, following the discovery of smelting and forging iron around 1200 B.C., spurred the invention of new types of metal tools. In the five centuries beginning around 600 B. C., such metal tools as tongs, shears, planes, scythes and spades were added to the kit inherited from the Stone and Bronze Ages.

In the Bronze Age civilizations production was predominantly for communal use and immediate local consumption. Trade was largely restricted to luxury articles which did not play a major role in economic life. With the advent of the Iron Age the division of labor became more complex. Many different kinds of craftsmen sprang up in the cities. The rapid growth of commerce spun a far-flung web of market relations which transformed the structures of the main maritime centers.

Agriculture had been virtually the sole mode of producing subsistence and wealth in the Bronze Age economies. Now manufacturing and trade acquired considerable, and in some key places decisive, importance for the first time. The progress and achievements of the Greek city-states were bound up with the development of their external trade. Commercial, shipping, manufacturing and colonizing enterprises brought them into connection with the most remote regions as well as with the most highly civilized states. Their diversified internal life was the offshoot of their participation in a market area which stretched from one end of the Mediterranean to the other and from Egypt to the Black Sea and which included the kingdoms of Mesopotamia.

Three epoch-making inventions, metallic money, alphabetic writing and weights and measures, made their appearance at this point. All were the result of the requirements of mercantile activities. Metallic money was invented at the beginning of the 8th Century on the boundaries of the Greek and Eastern worlds. The earliest coins facilitated the exchange relations of Lydia with the Greek ports. Alphabetic writing was developed and diffused for the sake of keeping commercial accounts. Stable systems of weights and measures were devised and established to promote the ready exchange of commodities.

Such innovations and economic changes created new social forces which in time effected a thorough reconstruction of social relations. The patriarchal slavery of Mesopotamia and Egypt was supplanted or supplemented by commercial slavery in which increasing numbers of bondsmen produced commodities for expanding markets and themselves became important commodities. Hereditary land-owning oligarchs living on self-contained estates became transformed into landed proprietors having extensive commercial connections with nearby or foreign markets. Laborers on their lands became converted from totally dependent serfs into small landowners. Shepherds came to tend flocks whose products also entered the channels of trade.

However, the biggest shifts in the social structure took place not in the countryside but in the ports. Cities emerged in which agricultural interests were no longer supreme but became subordinate to commercial and manufacturing interests. In these places independent merchant aristocracies, whose wealth was derived not from catering to monarchs, nobles and priests but from far-flung markets rose up alongside increasingly independent craftsmen and seafarers.

These newly enriched merchants, shipowners, financiers and manufacturers challenged the domination of the old landed and military aristocracies and toppled the representatives of the archaic order one by one. First to be abridged were the powers of the absolute monarchies. Along with them the priesthoods, which were omnipotent in Egypt and Babylonia, became demoted to dependent institutions. Finally, the mercantile, manufacturing and maritime interests came to grips with the landed nobility.

New forms of government replaced the absolute despotisms and landed oligarchies as a result of these struggles. These took the shape of constitutional monarchies, tyrannies, oligarchies, and, most notably, democratic republics. New forms of law emerged along with them. The customary codes inherited from primitive tribalism no longer fitted the needs or satisfied the demands of the mercantile elements who desired a better administration of justice and enforcement of contracts as well as a more favorable division of political rights.

The new conditions of urban life upset deep-rooted moral ideas and values. Hitherto birth and family connections had been the basis of status. Now citizens came to be judged and esteemed not for birth and pedigree alone but for their wealth and income. "Money makes the man."

The upper circles of the Ionian seaports displayed a practical worldly wisdom worthy of Benjamin Franklin's Poor Richard. "Get your living—and then think of getting virtue," wrote a 6th Century poet of Miletus. In his only surviving verse the Ionian poet Pythermus asserted: "There's nothing else that matters—only money."

The supreme outcome of all these revolutionary changes was the production of new forms of general consciousness. Magic was the characteristic world-view of tribalism; religion of the earliest kingdoms and city-states. Now something genuinely new emerged in the practice and minds of men: the first shoots of philosophy and science.

These could not have appeared until the historical soil for their growth and cultivation had been prepared and enriched by the elements we have described: the introduction of iron, metallic money, alphabetic writing, weights and measures; a new type of slave production; the shattering of the remaining institutions of tribal society and the breakup of agriculturally based theocratic despotisms; the ascent of trade, manufacturing and colonizing to new levels; the birth of powerful new progressive social forces in the maritime city-states of Greece which carried class antagonisms to a new pitch of intensity and created new types of legal, political and cultural institutions. Such were the indispensable historical preconditions for the formation of philosophy.

◰ The Ionian City-States

THESE HISTORICAL CONDITIONS also gave birth to a new type of city-state which differed in decisive respects from the older urban centers which had flourished for several thousand years in the cradles of civilization.

The cities of Mesopotamia and Egypt were located in river valleys. Their agricultural economies depended upon close and constant control of the water supply and waterways. These were held and maintained by highly centralized governments headed by absolute monarchs, priestly castes and nobles. The conservative theocratic kingdoms exercised the same thoroughgoing sway over men's minds through the religions administered by their priests as they did over men's lives and livelihoods through their bureaucratic officialdoms.

The principal buildings of these cities were representative of their social structure. Farrington has well said: "Ziggurats, pyramids, temples, palaces, colossal statues—the dwellings, tombs and images of kings and gods—apprise us of the organizing ability of the great, the technical skill of the humble, and the superstitions on which society was based."

The new Greek cities which arose on the shores of Asia Minor around the 8th Century B.C. drew upon the achievements of their forerunners. But they had many novel features in their background and make-up which marked them off from the older urban centers.

The Ionian city-states comprised a unique blending of social elements drawn from four sources. First, they retained many of the customs, traits and institutions which the Greeks had brought along with them from the higher stages of barbarism. Second, these were combined with vestiges of the Minoan-Mycenean civilizations. Then these elements from the older Aegean cultures became fused with acquisitions from the neighboring peoples of the East. Finally, all these were remolded according to the requirements of their maritime commercial activities.

The Ionian Greeks were apt and gifted pupils of the higher cultures around them, which they quickly surpassed. They resemble the American imitators of Western Europe, the Japanese assimilators of capitalism, or the contemporary Chinese emulators of Soviet accomplishments. The Ionian settlements were composed of emigrants of diverse origins from numerous regions who had been uprooted from their pasts and were less bound by tradition. The Greek migrants entered into friendly relations with the native peoples with whom they intermingled and intermarried.

They were favored by an excellent climate and good harbors. The city inhabitants had easy access to the products of field and pasture in the hinterland settled by farmers and herdsmen. By land they had intercourse with the Eastern monarchies and the Lydian-Phrygian kingdoms with which they exchanged goods for food and raw materials. From the Lydians they received a system of weights and measures and learned the use of money.

This mixture of emigrant Greeks and native peoples, submitted to the influences of Eastern and Hellenic cultures, were the first to create a common language, religious associations, interests, ideas and culture among the Greeks, thereby paving the way for the formation of a distinctively Greek nationality.

Through colonial settlements and the development of home industry the Ionians built up thriving centers of trade and manufacture linked with many other peoples by land and by sea. Their ships took the produce of Greek agriculture: oil and wine, and of Greek industry: arms, pottery, jewelry, clothing, and received in return grain, fish, wood, wool, metals and slaves.

The Ionians were enterprising negotiators, hardy sailors, daring navigators, explorers and adventurers. Thales, like Solon of Athens as Aristotle described him, went to Egypt "to do business and see the world." In that period shipbuilding occupied the same central place in technology that the construction of locomotives did in the early 19th Century. As maritime and naval powers, the Ionians produced skillful shipbuilders as well as able engineers who constructed harbors, bridges and tunnels.

In Mesopotamia and Egypt monarchs, priests and nobles had dominated dependent artisans and sluggish masses of feudal and slave laborers on the land. The Ionian cities were ruled by alert and cultured commercial aristocracies and crowded with clever craftsmen, ship artisans and robust mariners. In their more diversified and advanced economies artisans as well as merchants and manufacturers acquired a higher status. The artisans of Babylon, Egypt and Crete used copper and bronze tools which were scarce, costly and not very durable. They were kept under the thumbs of the potentates and priests in whose hands the food supplies were concentrated.

The Greek craftsmen were children of the Iron Age. The more plentiful, inexpensive and enduring metal made it possible for them to possess their own kit of tools and control both their productive activities and means of production. They were familiar with kings, nobles and priests. But since many worked in their own quarters on their own account for extensive and growing markets at home and abroad, they were far less dependent upon the palaces and citadels of kings, the households of nobles and the temples of the priesthoods around which the older cities revolved. These conditions of life and labor gave the city workmen a greater sense of independence, initiative and individuality which was matched by the sailors and longshoremen of their home towns.

These cities contained other classes in addition to the nobility, the merchants, the small shopkeepers, artisans and maritime workers. There were foreigners who had no civic rights and slaves without any rights whatsoever.

Slaves were traded and employed in various capacities. But slavery was not so dominant in the agricultural or industrial life of the Ionian cities of the 6th Century as it became in the Athens of the 4th Century. Many of the manufactures for export were fabricated by freemen. Slavery did not choke off the development and activities of the independent craftsmen nor did it lift the merchants far above the domain of production. The merchants kept their fingers closely on the pulse of industry and were well acquainted with its functioning.

When we think today of ancient Greece, we usually assume that Athens and Sparta were its capitals from the start. This is not so. These places on the mainland did not acquire their hegemony until the 5th or 4th Centuries B.C. While they were still immature in their social development during the 7th and 6th Centuries, the Greek settlements along the coast of Asia Minor were highly advanced.

It was not the cities of Greece proper which brought enlightenment to the outlying colonies; it was the Asian outposts which were the leaders and educators of metropolitan Greece. They not only elevated the mainland Greeks but helped civilize the barbarians around them.

In their technology and economy, their social constitution, their political activities, their culture and ideas, the Ionians were far ahead of the other Greeks in the 6th Century. They were the commercial pacemakers of Aegean civilization. Miletus was the most progressive center in the whole Greek world at that time. It was the mother city of ninety colonies around the Black Sea; its trade extended far and wide over the Mediterranean; its inhabitants were in contact with all the older hearths of civilization.

The Ionians not only took the lead in colonization and navigation, in the arts and crafts, in architecture and engineering. Greek art and literature as well as science and philosophy were born and bred in these Ionian cities. There the Homeric poems were polished into their perfected versions; there Sappho, Anacreon and others wrote their imperishable lyrics. The Ionians likewise fashioned the first instruments of prose writing for the Greeks.

The Mesopotamian and Egyptian civilizations were unmitigated despotisms. The monarchy as an institution was never abolished in these empires. The flourishing maritime cities of Ionia had a different political evolution and character. They were independent states, each with its own government. Originally they had been ruled by hereditary kings who were replaced by aristocracies of birth. By the middle of the 7th Century these in turn began to be ousted by coalitions of shipowners, merchants and manufacturers whose power was based not on landed property but on movable wealth. Growing trade not only strengthened the numbers, income and influence of the mercantile classes but broke up the cohesion of the old landed aristocracies as many noblemen entered business or established profitable connections with tradesmen.

In these free, independent and relatively democratic cities class struggles came to be waged openly and vigorously. The 6th Century saw the rise of a novel political phenomenon: the tyrannies. The tyrants were mostly merchant princes, somewhat like the Medici family of Florence, who took advantage of the turmoil of class conflicts to place themselves at the head of the popular forces and seize power.

With the transition from agricultural self-sufficiency to a money economy, the swift development of commodity production, the extension of trade and the accumulation of monied wealth, the new merchant class entered the lists to combat the kings and nobles who drew their privileges from birth and their wealth from landed estates. The tyrants were not poor commoners; they usually belonged to one of the contending factions among the upper classes. But to achieve power for their interests and to hold it, they were obliged to range themselves alongside the urban plebeians and the dispossessed and discontented peasantry and sponsor certain of their demands.

"Aristotle states that most tyrants gained their position by taking the side of the people against the rich nobles, a cause for which opportunities were likely to arise in such a city as Miletus, where manufactures played an important part, and the people were consequently more likely to realize their own importance than was the case in purely agricultural communities. Moreover, there must have been constant fluctuations in wealth among the merchant nobles, and therefore the power of that body would be less firmly established than it would have been had it depended on the possession of land in a state where there was no other source of wealth, either industrial or commercial. Consequently, though the commons did not necessarily become supreme, they were a force in the state, and were able to secure the elevation of their own champion to the position of power, first as chief magistrate and then as tyrant."—*The History of Miletus,* by Adelaide Glynn Dunham (pp. 126-127).

The tyrants thus became for a time popular heroes and champions of the masses. It is paradoxical but true that democracy and civic liberty entered the Western world under the auspices of these aspiring dictators who had many brilliant regimes to their credit. But the Greek plebeians never completely reconciled themselves to the sovereignty of these self-made autocrats and with a new turn in the class struggle the slayers of tyrants became regarded as heroes and saviors of democracy by the populace.

The tyrannies were intermediate formations in the political evolution of the Greek city-states. "The function of the Greek tyranny was transitional," George Thomson has pointed out. "By forcing and holding a breach in the rule of the aristocracy, it enabled the middle class to consolidate its forces for the final stage in the democratic revolution which involved the overthrow of the tyranny itself. That is why in Greek tradition, it was almost unanimously condemned. It was denounced in advance by the aristocrats because it was progressive, and in retrospect by the democrats because it had become reactionary."—*Aeschylus and Athens* (p. 93).

Thus the revolution in intellectual outlook which produced philosophy had been preceded by revolutionary changes in the economic foundations of Greek life through which aggressive and progressive trading centers inhabited by contending social classes replaced self-sufficing agricultural communities based upon tribal, clan and family ties. It was likewise attended by revolutionary upheavals in the political regime where merchants upset the power of the landed nobility and tyrants opened the gates for the democratic thrust of the plebeians. The driving forces for the forward movements of this age in almost all fields from technology to philosophy came from the merchant classes associated with the artisans and mariners of the cities.

▣ Miletus: The Birthplace of Philosophy

TODAY MILETUS IS NOT world-renowned like Babylon, Athens and Rome. Nor, except to students of philosophy, is its name so familiar as Sparta's or even the Phoenician cities of Tyre and Sidon. Yet it deserves a rank equal to the greatest of these.

Miletus was the birthplace of philosophy. All the historical factors which distinguished the progress of Asia Minor from the 8th to the 5th Centuries were most fully developed in this seaport. Miletus was characteristized by Herodotus as the "ornament of Ionia." In Roman times it still boasted of being "the most ancient city of Ionia, and the mother of many great cities on the Euxine, in Egypt, and in every region of the inhabited world."

The following description of the city in its prime by a French scholar, A. Jardé, is worth quoting at length. "Built on a peninsula nearly two miles long and of an average breadth between half and two-thirds of a mile, it offered all the advantages sought by the Greek colonist, being separated from the mainland by an isthmus closed by high ramparts, and communicating with the sea by four large bays which were all safe shelters. The heart of the city was the great northeast harbor, with two colossal lions guarding the entrance, three lines of wharves and porticoes along the sides, and the shrine of the Delphinian Apollo, the

68

ancient protector of sailors and emigrants, over-looking all.

"From here the Milesian ships sailed in every direction, an innumerable merchant navy, protected by a powerful war fleet. At the battle of Lade, Miletos brought 80 ships into action—only less than 100 ships from Chios. To feed her trade, she had created an industry. She had learned from the Lydians the art of weaving and dyeing fabrics and decorating garments and carpets. The woolens of Miletos were greatly prized in Athens and found buyers as far as Southern Italy; the cloak of Antisthenes of Sybaris, with its zones of flowers and figures, was a masterpiece of embroidery in the Oriental style.

"On all the markets of the Mediterranean Milesian traders were to be found. Miletos did business with the commercial cities of Euboea, and was involved in the war between Chalcis and Eretria. Through the colonies which she had founded from the Hellespont to the Caucasus, she had a monopoly of trade on the Euxine (Black Sea), or something very near it. Though she had no colonies in the Western Mediterranean, like Phocaea, she maintained commercial relations with the cities of Great Greece; the destruction of Sybaris affected Miletos like a national disaster. Her merchants visited the Etruscan ports constantly; and until 480, the goods and vases of Attica were imported into Etruria exclusively by Ionians.

"Phocaea, Ephesos, and the other great towns of Ionia, peopled, like Miletos, by a busy throng of merchants, craftsmen, and sailors, were all the scene of the like activity and the like wealth. Everywhere

there was the same taste for luxury, the same love of
fine fabrics and rich jewels; everywhere there were the
same banquets and festivals. The courtesans of Ionia
were models of elegance and culture, and all antiquity
would marvel at the friend of Pericles, Milesian Aspasia.
Xenophanes of Colophon shows us his fellow-towns-
men strolling on the Agora, 'clad all in purple, with
their hair beautifully dressed, shedding the perfume
of subtle ointments.' "—*The Evolution of the Greek
People* (pp. 193-194).

This citation depicts the upper classes of Miletus.
But in addition to "the swells": nobles, rich merchants,
shipowners and their elegant courtesans and refined
ladies, there were thousands of artisans, craftsmen,
waterfront workers and sailors at work and their
families at home in this busy maritime city-state.

Miletus had a long commercial history; it was pos-
sibly once a Cretan trading post. The Greeks had
arrived there ten centuries before Christ with Athenians at their head. Athens regarded Miletus as her
offspring. The city first rose to prominence at the beginning of the 8th Century when the Phoenicians were
driven from Greek waters and the Ionians took over
their functions as traders. Miletus was exceptionally
well-fitted to become the paramount seaport on the
Gulf of Latmos which formed the natural center for
the maritime trade of the Eastern Aegean. Built on a
promontory jutting out into the sea, its harbors at the
mouth of the Meander River had exceptional facilities for handling sea-borne traffic.

It was in the best position for the north and west
trade routes. Unlike other cities on the coast, it was

not dependent for its prosperity upon caravan trading but upon sea-borne commerce. It became the chief distributing center for the Eastern Aegean and the intersection of its trade.

Miletus was the first Greek city to use coined money and it became the richest as well as the most cultured city of Ionia. The Temple of Apollo at Didyma within its territory was not only a central shrine of worship for the entire region but also its bank. The temple authorities minted coins, held deposits, and superintended colonizing expeditions.

The Milesians became masters of the Aegean Sea and its trade. In connection with the thriving export business which was the main source of their wealth, the city had extensive manufactures. Its woolen trade was as famous in the 6th Century B.C. as those of the Florentines and Flemish in the Middle Ages. Its textile workshops fabricated quality goods for aristocrats, fine tissues artistically decorated with many-colored embroideries. From the Angora wool and flax raised in the countryside its craftsmen wove hangings, carpets, chlamys and cloaks. Fulling and dyeing were allied and prosperous crafts. Milesian woolens were exported as far as Italy.

Its pottery, a ware of reddish clay with light yellow coating, was sold from the Black Sea to Italy. The manufacture of pottery went hand in hand with the olive oil industry, another branch of its export trade. From nearby mines Miletus secured a plentiful supply of iron both for home use and export together with quantities of silver and gold for monetary use.

Its manufacturing activities were closely bound up

with trade in agricultural produce. The Milesians grew corn, olives, Smyrna figs, flax for clothing, made honey and wax, extracted purple dyes, sold fresh and salted fish, wine and olive oil. From their stock breeding came hides and Angora wool. They had an extensive woodworking industry, providing timber for their ships and furniture for export.

Slaves were another big commodity. Their traders obtained slaves from the Black Sea and Asia Minor and distributed them throughout Greece.

Thanks to its favored situation and booming agricultural and industrial activities, its maritime expansion was unparallelled in the history of any Greek state. Miletus took the lead in colonizing the Black Sea region. To the barbarous inhabitants around the many trading posts on its shores the Milesians carried the goods, customs and ideas of civilization and returned with the natural products of the region for their consumption and commerce. Fish, salt, wool, hides, corn, timber, iron, silver and gold, red earth for paint, vegetable dyes and slaves were the chief imports.

At Berezan, an island of fishermen in the Black Sea supplied with food by the Milesians, almost everyone could read and write, and among the merchants who covered themselves with gorgeous jewelry it was the correct thing to give orders to Athenian artists. Although Miletus founded no colonies in the Western Mediterranean, it had extensive trade connections there, as Jardé points out.

Not only was the mother city a bustling seaport but its extensions in Egypt and the Black Sea were filled with polyglot populations active in the comings and goings involved in busy trading towns.

When the Sait dynasty opened Egypt for the first time to merchants and settlers from Greece in the 7th Century, the Milesians sailed into the mouth of the Nile with 30 ships and built the so-called Milesian wall at Naucratis, the only place where Greeks were allowed to settle. Although they later had bazaars at Memphis and Abydos, Naucratis became the principal source of exchange of goods and ideas between the Egyptians and Greeks. After 569, special temples and quays were reserved for the Milesians; they enjoyed undisputed preeminence in that place. Naucratis became the chief market of Egypt and one of the most thriving in the whole Greek world; there the produce of Africa and Arabia was exchanged for Greek wares. The respect of the Egyptians for Miletus can be seen in the act of the Egyptian king Necho who, after his victory over Josiah of Juda, sent his battle accoutrements to Didyma as an offering to Apollo.

These economic developments gave immense wealth and influence to the merchant class of Miletus and its colonies. King Croesus of Lydia, for instance, came to its millionaires for funds. These keen, adventurous, enlightened men not only fulfilled economic functions but held office as chief magistrates and high priests.

The Milesian merchants drew large revenues from stock-breeding. This resulted in a crumbling of the barriers between the base and the well-born and the merging of nobles with businessmen into a plutocracy. Active and intelligent landowners went into industry and commerce while the merchants penetrated their

ranks, either themselves becoming landed proprietors or establishing family or business connections
with them.

The merchants and shipowners had equally ambivalent relations with the crews of shipbuilders, wharf
workers and sailors who constituted a plebeian force
of considerable dimensions. Miletus is one of the first
places on record where maritime workers made their
mark as an energetic revolutionary force.

The masses of Miletus were a mobile, even mercurial,
body, composed of varied elements. There were artisans, craftsmen, seamen; many foreigners, some attracted by the trade opportunities, others homeless
who had drifted and congregated there; ruined peasants
uprooted from the land by the money economy; and
hordes of slaves of different nationalities. Like Athens
later, the city was the arena of intense and prolonged
class conflicts resulting in frequent overturns of political regimes. It was often involved in commercial wars
against expanding rivals such as Samos, Corinth
and Colchis.

By the 8th Century the original hereditary monarchy
had been overthrown by a landowning aristocracy.
This was in turn challenged and supplanted by the
rule of the rich merchants in the middle of the 7th
Century. Miletus soon became the classical seat of
the tyranny. By 604 B. C. the noted tyrant Thrasy-
bulus had taken power. But the regimes of the tyrants,
though brilliant, were short lived. The last two tyrants
were driven out about 580 B. C.

After their expulsion, Miletus was plunged into two
generations of violent civil strife in which power fluc-

tuated between the parties of the rich on one side and the plebeian "hand-workers" on the other. At first the poor were triumphant; then the rich regained their supremacy. The outcome was a compromise: the establishment of a moderate oligarchy composed of wealthy merchants and prosperous farmers with restricted powers. The magistrates, for example, held office for only two months.

This was not the end of governmental changes. The constitutional regime was overthrown by a new tyranny. This was replaced by a democratic government which ruled until the city fell to the Persians after the conquest of Lydia in 546. The Persians destroyed the city after crushing an Ionian revolt led by the Milesians in 494; it never regained its former importance.

Thus, during most of its existence as the foremost city of the Aegean, Miletus was governed by the well-to-do who were periodically fought and at times dislodged from leadership by the plebeians. But the plebeian democracy could never perpetuate its rule or keep it from slipping back to the merchant princes.

One cause for this political instability was the fact that the sailors, the most militant segment of the democratic forces, had to embark periodically on long voyages, whereas the merchants and their supporters could stay home. For the same occupational reason maritime workers have usually been a more inflammable but less steady support for radical movements than the urban artisans.

The Milesians made the most of the cultural innovations of the young Iron Age. Reading and writing, which democratized knowledge as iron democratized the use of metal, was widespread among its citizens. The keeping of accounts fostered habits of precision and stimulated the capacities for generalizing thought. Upon the foundation of such an alert and literate citizenry Miletus became the intellectual as well as the commercial and manufacturing capital of the civilized world at that time.

VI. The First Philosophers

THE FIRST PHILOSOPHERS, THE
so-called "naturalists" of Miletus, rose up out of the
free-thinking, wide-ranging merchant class or from
landed patricians influenced by their ways. From antiquity to the bourgeois era the merchant class has
produced many outstanding thinkers in various fields.

Nowadays we are accustomed to picture philosophers
as detached from practical affairs. The earliest Greek
thinkers did not at all resemble professors in academic
cloisters. They were active and prominent citizens of
their communities who engaged in business enterprises
and political life, travelled to foreign lands, and promoted technical knowledge as well as generalized
thought.

The founder of the Milesian school was Thales
(c. 624—548-45 B.C.) who headed the list of "the
seven wise men of Greece." According to Aristotle,
he was a shrewd businessman who once made a lot

of money by using his knowledge of the stars to antic-
ipate a great harvest of olives, acquire all the olive
presses in Chios and Miletus, and corner the market
at harvest time. This anecdote is significant because
it unwittingly points up the connection between the
scientific and economic activities of the Ionians. Thales
urged the Ionian cities to unite in a federal council
against their Persian foes—and some of his disciples
took part in the democratic struggles of their day.

The merchant class had a strong material interest
in mathematics, astronomy, meteorology and geography because of their value in navigation. Where fortunes were made or lost in shipping and lives were
risked in difficult voyages, it was imperative to study
weather conditions, know the stars and the tides,
ascertain the location of ships at sea and the peculi-
arities of harbors. Like the scientists of early republican New England, who came mostly from the coastal
towns, the Milesian wise men sought to assist seafarers by studying climate and heavenly phenomena.
Their scientific inquiries were stimulated and guided
by the demands of commercial shipping.

Thales was the first Greek astronomer and the first
Greek mathematician; he was also reputed to be
the discoverer of the magnetic property of the lode-
stone. The force he saw at work is today regarded as
the inner constitution of matter. He is said to have
learned improvements in the art of navigation from
the Phoenicians. Anaximander is supposed to have
made the first map of the known world and to have
imported the sundial from Egypt to measure the
passage of time. He maintained that the world was

round and was the first to explain that the light of the moon was borrowed from the sun. Hecataeus, who belonged to an ancient Milesian family, became "the father of geography" thanks to his travels and the information he amassed from the sailors and merchants of his home town.

These achievements and the stories associated with them testify to the readiness of the Milesians to assimilate and develop whatever they learned from other peoples. They likewise demonstrate how closely their scientific work and philosophical speculations were tied up with their commercial and industrial life.

The practical activities of the Milesians were not only responsible for the direction of their scientific discoveries but also for the special traits of their thinking. Kautsky has explained how trade gives rise to ways of thinking different from those based on handicraft and agriculture. The thought processes and ideas of the craftsmen and peasant are very concrete but extremely narrow.

"The activity of the merchant on the other hand has a quite different effect on him. He need not confine himself to the knowledge of a specific branch of production in a specific locality; the wider his view, the more branches of production he takes in, the more regions with their special needs and conditions of production, the sooner he will find out which commodities it is most profitable to deal in at a given time; the sooner he will find the markets where he can buy most profitably and those in which he can sell most profitably. For all the diversity of products and markets he is involved in, basically his interest is only in the relationship of prices, that is, the relationships of various quantities of abstract human labor, that is, of abstract numerical relationships. The more trade develops, the more buying and selling are separate in space and time, the greater the differences of the coins and coinages the merchant has to deal with, the further apart the acts of selling and payment are and systems of credit and interest develop: the more complex and diversified these numerical relationships become. Thus trade must develop mathematical thinking and, along with that, abstract thinking.

"As trade broadens horizons beyond local and professional narrowmindedness and opens up to the merchant knowledge of the most differing climates and soils, stages of culture and modes of production, it stimulates him to comparisons, enables him to see what is general in the mass of particulars, what is regular in the mass of fortuities, what always repeats itself under given conditions. In this way, as well as by mathematical thinking, the power of abstraction is highly developed, while handicrafts and arts develop the sense for the concrete, but also for the superficial aspects, rather than the essence of things. It is not the 'productive' activities like agriculture and handicrafts, but 'unproductive' trade that forms the mental capacities that constitute the basis of scientific research."—*Foundations of Christianity* (pp. 166-167).

Kautsky adds the qualification that, in addition to trading, leisure time is required for disinterested research and scientific thought. "Trade develops the requisite mental traits but not their application in science," and he goes on to observe that "scientific thought could only arise in a class that was influenced by all those traits, experiences and knowledge that trade brought with it, but at the same time was free from the need of earning money and so had time and opportunity for, and joy in unprejudiced research, in solving problems without considering their immediate, practical and personal results." This was provided by the class of affluent landholders who dwelt in the maritime trading cities or were immersed in their culture.

The spread of literacy through the invention of the alphabet gave no less an impetus to abstract thought than the habits of dealing in commodities, calculating prices and casting up accounts. Alphabetic writing was not only more easily popularized; it was a more generalized form of expressing ideas. The written word represented a higher degree of abstraction than the previous forms of writing in pictographs and ideographs, which professional scribes had monopolized. The letters of the alphabet, like the letters later used in algebra, are meaningless in themselves; they serve to designate the smallest phonetic elements to which the words can be reduced. By thus objectifying speech in written form the Greeks obtained acquaintance with the structural elements of their language and began to analyze the meaning of terms and the functions of parts of speech. They became rhetoricians, grammarians and logicians.

For these cultural and material reasons the urge to philosophize was first felt among communities with an eagerly inquisitive as well as acquisitive merchant class, enlightened elements among a landed aristo-

cracy, alongside a free, active and independent mass
of artisans and seamen, who not only contended with
one another for power but mutally influenced one
another.

Twenty-four hundred years later something analogous was produced on a higher historical basis in the
era of commercial capitalism among the maritime
merchants and plantation owners of colonial North
America who supplied the leaders and ideologists of
the First American Revolution. It is not far fetched to
view Thales as a sort of Ionian Benjamin Franklin,
that many-sided American who was a printing craftsman, a businessman, statesman and diplomat, bon-
vivant, writer, economist, inventor, moralist, and
scientist. Anaximander recalls Thomas Jefferson who
not only superintended his plantation and built a
new nation but was interested in agricultural innovations, architecture, education, the reform of religion
and many other matters.

The positive conditions which bred the first philosophers, scientists and materialists are to be found in
the economic activities which induced the Milesians
to give close and constant attention to the problems
of technology and to such sciences as astronomy,
geometry, meteorology and biology. Class conflicts
stimulated their energies and fostered a keen sense
of individuality and civic liberty. But there were other
peculiar features of the city which made it possible for
freedom of thought to flourish.

Just as there was no absolute monarchy to impose
a rigid system of government upon a subject people,
so the priesthood was in no position to manacle the

minds of men by superstition and prevent inquiry into social and natural processes. The temple oracle of Didyma administered by the hereditary priests of the cult of Apollo did not overshadow the city, master it or restrict the freedom of thought and action of its citizens. On the contrary, as its first mint and bank, the temple served the commercial interests of the community and promoted its colonizing enterprises. The influence it exercised all the way from Persia through Egypt to the Western Mediterranean was a factor in the greatness of Miletus.

In the 6th Century the dictator Histaeus proposed that the treasure of Apollo at the temple of Didyma be used to equip a fleet to fight the Persians. Even though this sacrilegious suggestion was rejected by the chief officials and high priests, it showed freedom from ecclesiastical tabus among the Milesians.

The Milesian naturalists were able to push their investigations in many directions without sacerdotal interference. The generalized upshot of their inquiries was the creation of a genuinely new method of thought, a new outlook upon the world, which marked the beginning of scientific insight into the nature of things.

Religion and Philosophy

"THE BEGINNING OF ALL criticism is the criticism of religion," observed Marx. This was so in the pioneering period of Greek thought. The Milesian criticism, or rather setting aside, of religious attitudes and ideas laid the foundations for philosophy and initiated the career of materialism.

As has been explained, for many thousands of years magical, animistic and religious conceptions of natural, social and mental processes had dominated and shaped men's minds. The religious viewpoint hinged upon acceptance of the existence and activities of super natural beings and powers.

Instead of giving a generalized definition of religion, let us dissect a typical sample of the ancient Greek religious outlook to see how divinity dominated their mental world. Homer's *Iliad* held a place in Greek education and imagination comparable to that of the Bible in the Western world. In the opening scene of the story Homer tells how the Greeks, encamped before Troy for ten years, have been struck by a plague. Many have died and dogs and kites have eaten their bodies lying on the ground.

Today epidemiologists would search for the natural causes and social circumstances of such an epidemic. But the Homeric Greeks believed the affliction to be a punishment for some unknown offense against a god. They did not ask: what bacteriological agents or living conditions caused this sickness, but which of the gods had been injured, by whom, and in what way?

Instead of calling upon research workers and physicians, they brought out a seer, the Hellenic counterpart of a medicine man or shaman. He reported that the angered god was Apollo who had retaliated by shooting magically invisible arrows from a silver bow into the camp. How had the Greeks offended this mighty divine chief?

Agamemnon, the Greek leader, had seized the daughter of a local caretaker of Apollo's shrine. Apollo had answered the prayers of his priest for revenge by bringing the plague upon the camp. Acting upon this diagnosis, the Greek generals forced Agamemnon to give up his concubine. Although this concession provoked dissension among the warring Greeks, it satisfied the priest and appeased Apollo who lifted the plague.

This is a specimen of primitive Greek religion. It is likewise pure magic, of the same kind believed and practiced today by the natives of West Africa or among the tribes of the upper Amazon. In fact, its ingredients had been handed down to Homer from the Stone Age of the Hellenic tribesmen.

The Milesian naturalists delivered a mortal blow to this magical method and mythological outlook by disposing of its very foundations. They went back to the beginning of all things and asked: what created the world and how was it done? In Homeric mythology the gods Oceanus and Tethys were the originators of all things, including the other gods.

The Babylonians and Egyptians had similar myths about the origin of the world which were rooted in their special historical experience. In both countries the land from which the people drew their sustenance had been wrested by desperate struggle from nature by draining the swamps beside the rivers. They therefore taught that the beginnings of things came about when a divine being did the equivalent of bidding: "Let the dry land appear."

The name of the Babylonian creator was Marduk. "All the lands were sea . . . Marduk bound a rush mat upon the face of the waters, he made dirt, and piled it beside the rush mat."

The birth of mankind was ascribed to a similar act of divine creation. According to the myths of the Israelites who lived in a nearby country around the same time, their tribal god, Jehovah, who is much more familiar to us, fashioned mankind as a brick-maker does bricks. He took a handful of dust and breathed life into it.

What did the first Greek materialists do that was so daring, progressive, and revolutionary? They gave an explanation of the formation of the world and of man which left out Oceanus, Marduk, Jehovah or any other godlike personage, magical power or spiritual agency.

Homer had attributed the origin of all things to the *god* Oceanus. Thales, the founder of materialism, taught that *water* is the origin of everything. There is something alike in these methods of explanation since both connect the beginning of things with this liquid. But there is a world of difference between the two.

In his theory the philosopher dispensed with any magical, mythical or allegorical agents. His primal substance is a visible part of the experienced world, a purely natural element. *Between the god Oceanus as the first parent, and water, the physical thing, as the basis of explanation, is the decisive shift from animism to materialism, from religion to philosophy.*

This same contrast stands out in respect to the Babylonian and Egyptian legends of the origins of things. Thales agreed with these that everything was once water. But he maintained, in opposition to them, that the earth and everything else had been formed out of water by purely natural processes, similar to the silting up of deltas at the mouth of rivers.

Anaximander, the next in line among the Milesian materialists, accounted for the birth of mankind in an equally natural way. He said that all living creatures emerged from the moist elements; fish had preceded land animals and man had once been like a fish. As the waters receded and dry land appeared, some fish had to adapt themselves to living on land and became men. He based his reasoning upon the observed fact that man is the only animal that requires a long period of suckling and could not have survived unless the species was nurtured by another. This was a speculation of genius, comparable to the atomic theory of the subsequent Greek materialists, for Anaximander's guess was not far from the true course of organic evolution.

What these original materialists did was to offer a coherent account, crude and inadequate as it was, of the creation of the world and of mankind without bringing in the gods or letting in any magical forces. This may not seem very remarkable today when it has become a commonplace. But 2,500 years ago it was epoch-making. Perhaps the following analogy will help highlight its revolutionary implications.

The religious cosmologists believed that it took both the gods and nature to make up the world. But the gods were the most essential and powerful of the two because they created and governed the world. So today the upholders of capitalism teach that society requires a ruling bourgeoisie on top and a working class on the bottom. A person is on the road to becoming a revolutionary socialist when he begins to understand that the parasitic capitalist class is superfluous to the further progress of society. Just as the socialist movement bases itself upon the exclusion of the exploiters from economic and political life and brings forward the real producers as the governing force, so the Ionians eliminated supernatural forces from their theories of nature and mankind and replaced them with genuine physical forces.

The extraordinary quality of the Milesian achievement can be gauged by noting that, during this same period, Judaism was emerging in Palestine, the religion of Zoroaster in Persia, Buddhism in India and Taoism and Confucianism in China. While these other peoples were producing new religions, the Ionians were breaking with the religious outlook altogether. The fact that the Persians and the Jews reformed polytheism by constructing a world-view around a single deity was undoubtedly a step forward. But they remained imprisoned within religious superstition.

The Milesians performed the incomparably greater feat of developing an explanation of things which didn't include a god at all. By rejecting all supernatural beings and forces and relying solely upon natural operations and physical processes in their theorizing, the Milesian materialists effected the most profound revolution in human thinking and started a wholly new method of understanding the universe and approaching its problems.

VII. The Milesian Contributions
to Materialism

OUR INFORMATION ABOUT
most Greek thinkers, and especially the earlier ones,
is very scanty. The accounts of their lives, works and
ideas are intermingled with legends. The extant texts
are fragmentary, distorted, contradictory and, even
with the most correct methods, lend themselves to divergent interpretations.

Nevertheless, the unanimous testimony of antiquity
is that the Milesians founded the first school of philosophy and placed it on a materialist basis. These
two facts are organically connected. It is essential to
understand why the birth of philosophy was likewise
the beginning of the materialist view of the world.
The position of the pioneer philosophers was determined by the nature of their opposition. The first form
of philosophical thought necessarily had to be materialist in its content because it was implicitly directed
against the dominant religious ideas and magical

methods constituted a critical opposition to them, and became the only solid alternative to them.

The method they introduced of explaining the for- mation of the world and its developments was the imperishable achievement of the Milesians. Instead of resorting to the gods as the creators and promoters of phenomena, they looked for the causes of things in the interconnections of events within nature and the interactions of natural elements alone.

Whereas the religous-minded spun narratives of what supposedly happened, the Milesian thinkers tried to single out from the welter of events around them in nature the decisive factors which brought things into being and made them what they are. This pro- cedure of searching for the explanation of things in the recurrences of nature and the laws of their move- ment, instead of in the actions and impulses of divine powers, was scientific in principle and rational in method.

In addition to their method of investigation, the Milesians made other important contributions to the materialist treasury.

One concerned the concept of matter itself. The Milesians did not arrive at any general idea of mat- ter; that was a later ideological development. But they initiated the train of speculation which culmin- ated in the definition of the category of matter.

The Milesians were compelled to consider the prob- lem of matter and its nature by the very starting point, momentum and direction of their thought. If the gods are rejected as the authors of events, then what in the world is the original source of all things? Aristotle, to whom we owe much of our information about their ideas, described the materialist conclusions of the Milesians in these words: "Most of the first philosophers thought the principle of all things was in the form of matter alone; for that out of which all things are and from which, as the first, they come into being, and into which, at the last, they pass away . . . this, they say is the element and the principle of things."

The lineage of Milesian thinkers was constituted by Thales, Anaximander, Anaximenes and Hecataeus. Although their mode of reasoning was the same, these various members of the Milesian school gave somewhat different answers to the question of what the specific form of matter was, what "the element and the principle of things" was. Thales singled out water as the primary substance from which all else was derived and to which it returns.

There are many conjectures why Thales took water as the primary stuff of nature, the essential reality of all other phenomena. Aristotle said that Thales saw the essential part played by water in nourishing life so that the hot element could come from it, since what is alive has heat. Water is also the essence of seeds. Aristotle also suggests that Thales might have been carrying forward the primacy that Greek and Egyptian mythology accorded water.

Later scholars have argued that Thales chose the moist element because of his special studies of climatic conditions. Water not only assumed such different forms as ice, liquid, and vapor but to the Greeks mist, wind, animal breath and life were all intermingled and identified. Whether meteorology, botany or biology, the phenomenon of evaporation, the germination of plants or the origin of life most inspired Thales, the reasons for his decision are not so important as the fact that he singled out a purely natural, physically observable element and used its properties and powers as the exclusive means of explaining reality.

Anaximander, his follower, took a step forward in developing the conception of matter. He objected to the notion of Thales that everything is essentially a form of water. He held that the primary substance could not be any specific element like water, or air, or fire. Aristotle sets forth his reasoning as follows: "They are in opposition one to another—air is cold, water moist and fire hot, and therefore, if any one of them is infinite, the rest would have ceased to be by this time." That is, one of the elements would have swallowed up all the others.

Anaximander taught that there must be something more primitive than any of these elements from which these warring opposites had separated out, to which they are attached, and into which they pass away. He called this substratum the boundless, the non-limited, the infinite. This non-limited was material and therefore perceptible but out of reach. It was apparently meant to designate the original stock of matter from which everything is derived. Anaximander had put his finger on the general category of matter, and especially on the inexhaustible creativity of matter which manifests itself in numberless forms but cannot be fixed or exclusively identified with any one of its determinations.

All the Milesians were cosmologists who sought to explain how the universe came into being and how the earth and the heavenly bodies were related. Thales said the earth floated in water. Anaximander gave a more elaborate account of the formation of the universe and its framework.

He took the four elements, earth, water, mist and fire, which the Greeks thought made up nature, to sketch the following evolution of the universe. The four elements were once on top of one another. The earth as the heaviest was at the center; water covered it; the mist was above the water; and fire, the lightest, embraced them all. The fire heated the water and caused it to evaporate. This made the dry land appear, but increased the volume of mist. When pressure grew to the breaking point, the fiery envelope of the universe burst and took the form of wheels of fire enclosed in tubes of mist circling around the earth and sea.

In terms of this scheme of natural evolution he attempted to give explanations of a number of astronomical and meteorological phenomena from the phases of the moon and its eclipses to the cause of thunder and lightning.

Anaximander's notion of the boundless extent of matter enabled him to make an advance in cosmology. He taught that there was more than one world. An unlimited number of universes had come into being and the process of their creation and dissolution never stopped. This doctrine of the plurality of worlds, which is essentially true, has an interesting history. It was taken up by the Atomists, set aside by the classical Greek idealists and the Christian theologians, and then came to the fore again with the Copernican revolution in astronomy and Bruno's speculations which spurred the revival of materialism at the dawn of the bourgeois era.

Anaximenes, the third luminary of the Milesian school, made still another advance in disclosing the modes of universal development. Neither Thales nor Anaximander had put forward any precise ideas on the nature of the physical processes by which the world was generated. Anaximenes sought to fill this gap. He settled upon mist as the first principle, or the primary substance, of all things. Air is always in motion, he said, because if it were not, it would not change so much as it does. (Both "mist" and "air" translate the Greek *aêr.*)

Anaximenes ascribed all changes in the cosmos to changes in the density of air. The different forms of things were the result of the looseness or compactness of their material composition brought about by the rarefaction and the condensation of the fundamental substance, air. Air transformed itself into fire, winds, earth or stones by becoming more closely packed like felt or by separating and flying apart.

He offered the following experiment as evidence of these universal processes. When we blow air from our mouths, it comes out cold if we purse our lips, press air down and make it compact. If we open our mouths wide and blow on our hands, the air expands and becomes hot. Processes like this compression and distention of air account for all the various phenomena.

His remarkable conception of what causes change and diversity in nature is a special application of the law of dialectics that quantitative changes bring about qualitative distinctions. For Anaximenes, variations in the density of the air generated the different kinds of matter. Thus a specific physical process by its action upon the original undifferentiated substance sufficed to account for the wide variety of things and even their opposing qualities.

These three thinkers engaged in a resolute, sustained and fruitful effort to trace everything back to their root causes in nature and to grapple with the analysis of the inner substance of matter. That search is still going on. But it was the Milesians who first embarked upon it and, with the instruments and knowledge at their disposal, headed in the right direction.

THE MILESIANS STUDIED THE
changes in things and tried to devise natural reasons
for the course of their development. They regarded
the universe as composed of four major elements:
earth, air, fire and mist. All the rest, the heavenly
bodies, the world, plants, animals and man, were in
one way or another derived from the interactions of
these elements.

But they did not offer any explanation of why
things had to change, why they could not remain as
they are. What was the mainspring of perpetual
change? The first answers to this problem are to be
found in the writings of an aristocrat from another
Ionian city, Heraclitus of Ephesus, who flourished
several generations after.

Heraclitus was one of the titans of human thought.
Hegel, a great thinker who knew the history of philosophy thoroughly, designated Heraclitus as the
originator of the laws of dialectics, and there is no
reason for depriving him of this honor. The old Greek
philosophers, said Engels, were all natural-born dia-
lecticians in their thinking. They were accustomed to
look upon phenomena as in constant change and in
perpetual development, to note their interconnections,
oppositions and contradictions, and their transitions
into something other than their original state.

This outstanding trait of Greek thought had one of

its most brilliant exponents in Heraclitus. He was the first theoretical analyzer of the general processes of change. He singled out fire as the first principle, the ultimate substance of things, from which all others are produced. Like the earlier Ionians he takes his stand upon materialist grounds. The following significant text from Heraclitus was preserved by Clement of Alexandria: "This world, which is the same for all things, was made by no god or man. It has always been, it is, and will be an ever-living fire, kindling with measure and being quenched with measure." Lenin described this as an "excellent exposition of the elements of dialectical materialism."

Heraclitus formulated two propositions which have become incorporated as pillars in the structure of dialectical thought. One was his doctrine that "everything flows." He gave picturesque examples of the universality of change. The sun is not only new every day but always continuously new. We cannot step twice into the same river for its waters are ever-flowing, ever-changing. All objects both are and are not; they are never the same but always changing into something else. By this reasoning Heraclitus dissolved all fixed states of being into the process of perpetual becoming in which every object enters existence, stays for a while and then passes away.

Heraclitus did more than state that everything is always on the go. He endeavored to explain why not even the most stable and solid substances could remain unaltered or at rest. Everything is composed of opposites, he said, which are always in a state of tension. Any given form of matter is the result of the balance of opposing forces within it.

This balance, however, is constantly being upset by the movement, the interaction, the contention of its warring opposites. All things are involved in a dual movement: one emanates from the oscillations generated by the interactions of the opposites within itself; the other from the movement of the whole either toward or away from its source. And one of these antagonistic forces is gaining on the other all the time until in the end it proves triumphant.

Pairs of opposites must be considered as internally unified, Heraclitus taught. Disease makes health pleasant; hunger brings satisfaction. He cited the screw and its movement to illustrate this unity of opposition. The screw engages in two opposite forms of movement at one and the same time: straight and crooked. The spiral motion characteristic of its function has a contradictory nature; it goes both around and up, rotating on the same plane and on a different one at the same time.

He presented still other examples of the opposition and identity of real contradictions. Things which are cut in opposite directions, like the mortise and tenon, he pointed out, fit together. The end and the beginning are opposites; yet they become one and are merged into each other in the circumference of the circle. A whole is made up of all its parts and all the parts come from a whole—and we can only know and understand the one and the many in relation to their generation from each other.

This law of the identity or interpenetration of

opposites as a primary feature of all things and as the explanation for their becoming and change we owe to Heraclitus. With its aid he was able to give a theoretical explanation both for the harmony and for the disruption of things, for their intimate interconnection and transition from one into the other.

"The fairest harmony is born of things different, and discord is what produces all things." Even the most harmonious and integrated unit cannot endure as such indefinitely because of the incessant movement of its opposites, the unbalancing of its contending inner forces. "Strife is the father of all things, the king of all things, and has made gods and men, free men and slaves."

This book will not dwell much on the dialectical method and its laws which I have written about elsewhere. Our chief concern in these pages is with the content and principles of materialism as they were developed in antiquity. But the teachings of Heraclitus demonstrate that the combined aspects of this philosophy—its materialist foundation and its dialectical method—were not solely the fruit of its ultimate stage of development but were implanted within it from the very beginning.

THE ATTENTION WHICH THE Milesians gave to the dialectical development of all things is manifested in another aspect of their view of matter, namely, its intrinsically dynamic character. The Milesians were called by the scholars of antiquity hylozoists, which, translated, means "those who think nature is alive."

The Milesians did not erect impassable barriers between nature, life, society and the human mind; they took for granted their essential unity and interconnections. They continued to clothe their conceptions of the dynamics of material processes in the old theological terms by saying that the gods were in everything. To them the gods represented the inner capacities for action. By saying that the gods were in everything these naturalists sought to diffuse throughout nature the power of initiating movement concentrated in divine beings alone.

Thus Aristotle declared that Thales apparently "admitted that the soul is a moving power, if it is true that he said of the loadstone that it has a soul because it moves iron." Later Xenophanes held that "God is the cause of motion."

Their emphasis upon the inherently dynamic quality of matter has considerable significance in the light of the subsequent course of Greek and European thought on this topic. Idealism later tended to deprive

101

matter of its inherent activity and to lodge the power of movement in forms, ideas, and spiritualized supreme beings. Matter was degraded until it came to be regarded as passive, inert, dead, a lower form of existence which owed its activity and movement to the external influence of forms, ideas, souls or God.

This conception of matter as essentially inert persisted and became part of the mechanical view of the world stemming from Galileo, Descartes, Newton and Locke. The separation of movement from matter with the correlative conception that motion is exclusively imparted by external agencies was defined by Kant in the 18th Century as follows: "The possibility of living matter cannot even be thought; its concept involves a contradiction because lifelessness, inertia, constitutes the essential character of matter."

If living matter is an absurdity, as Kant contended, then materialism is equally absurd and impossible. But the Milesians were not bothered by this alleged absolute dualism of matter and movement brought about by the subsequent development of theory. They looked upon nature as self-moving, and even as essentially alive, and did not counterpose passive matter to some other extraneous source of activity.

They were essentially correct, as against Kant, in spontaneously assuming that matter and motion were inseparable. What they failed to see was that matter is not necessarily, or even normally, the scene of lifelike phenomena. Life is a special form of motion, exceptionally existing and manifested in higher organizations of matter. But matter is always in motion and motion is always expressed in the action of something material.

Greek religion regarded the heavenly bodies and the heavens themselves as divine and therefore of a wholly different and higher order of being from anything on earth. The idealists were later to reinforce this dualism of existence by counterposing eternal forms and ideas to perishable matter; immortal gods to mortal men; divine souls to carnal bodies. This was foreign to the thought of the Milesian naturalists. They were monistic thinkers in contrast to the dualistic religious folk around them and the idealists who came after them. They spontaneously assumed the substantial unity of all things as an integral part of their outlook.

⟐ The Process of Evolution

FINALLY, THE MILESIANS were as evolutionary as they could be under the given conditions in their approach to the phenomena of nature and human life. They looked upon the forms of being from the standpoint of their becoming, their course of development, their passing away and their transformation into other things. We have already observed how their speculations on the origin and development of the universe were permeated with the spirit of the evolutionary method.

Let us review Anaximander's scheme. From the first indeterminate matter, the boundless, the two original contraries of heat and cold are differentiated through their own energy. What is cold settles down to the center and forms the earth; what is hot ascends to the circumference and originates the bright, shining, fiery bodies of heaven. These stars are fragments of what once existed as a complete shell which in time burst and broke up.

These speculations were crude, corresponding to the state of scientific knowledge at the time. But they do not differ in principle from the nebular hypothesis developed by Kant and LaPlace in the 18th Century or the more informed speculations on the origins of the stars and planets of today. The birth processes of the stars is a problem which has still to find its definitive solution.

Anaximander carried forward his description of the evolutionary process to explain the origins of life and of man. He said that the action of the sun's heat on the watery earth next generated films or bladders out of which came different kinds of imperfectly organized beings. These gradually developed into the animals now living. Man's ancestors were fishlike creatures which dwelt in muddy waters and only as the sun slowly dried up the earth did they become gradually fitted for life on dry land. Here is a comprehensive, well-thought-out, step-by-step explanation of the sequence of the origination of the universe, of life and mankind.

As the gods are thrust into the background, the interplay of nature and mankind comes forward more prominently and more powerfully. This can be seen in the Milesian speculations on the problem of biology and the development of mankind. Anaximander said that mankind arose from the moist element and was once like a fish. Anaxagoras, his successor, made a no less noteworthy contribution to materialism. He attributed the superiority of man over the other animals to his technological activity. According to him, man is the most intelligent of the animals because he had hands, the hand being the tool par excellence and the model of all tools.

This observation is wholly in line with the first principle of historical materialism which singles out the hand as the most important single biological organ responsible for the transformation of the primate into man because it made labor possible. The hand was the biological handle, the parent and prototype of the tool, and made possible both tool-using and tool-making.

▣ Shortcomings of the Milesians

ENOUGH EVIDENCE HAS BEEN given to demonstrate how materialist-minded the first philosophers among the Milesians were in their starting point, their procedures, and their conclusions. At the same time it must be noted that in many respects their ideas were misty, confused and erroneous. They were pioneers who could do no more than sketch the first rough approximation to a materialist interpretation of the universe.

Many old beliefs and absurdities were intermingled with their genuinely new, valid and fruitful insights. They saw the principle of activity as essentially divine and even thought of clouds as living things. They identified the wind with the breath of life. They still personified forces of nature, invoking such personal and social phenomena as love, hate and justice to explain the movements of things.

This is not surprising or to their discredit. All philosophies have to be approached as historical productions and judged not by timeless and arbitrary standards but according to the concrete conditions of their time and place. Each one is a combination of ideas which have been drawn from diverse sources and are of unequal value. After appraising the school of thought as an integrated unit, it is necessary to submit its varied content to critical dismemberment, analyze its components, sift the wheat from the chaff, and

106

measure their relative weights. Philosophies have to be judged not only by what they are in themselves but also by what they have come out of and what they gave birth to.

William Ellery Leonard has rightly remarked: "To appraise the science of the Greeks, we must begin not with man's knowledge after the Greeks but with man's ignorance before the Greeks." The same is true of the first philosophers.

The vestiges of old beliefs to be found in the Milesian thinkers signify only that they could not go farther than the scientific knowledge and social framework of their epoch permitted. It would be unhistorical, unrealistic and unreasonable to expect them to have done more.

They stand at the entry of philosophic inquiry. What is most significant about any school of philosophy is not the points where it stood still or retrogressed (although these have to be taken into account) but its vital, dynamic, creative sides. These are the places where it evolved something new which went beyond the ideas of its predecessors and thereby promoted the progress of human thought. The Milesians easily pass such a test.

⌑ Materialism and Atheism

THESE CONSIDERATIONS HAVE to be kept in mind as a guide in appraising their attitude toward the gods. It is now recognized, both by defenders of the faith and the advocates of materialism, that the materialist standpoint is essentially hostile to religion and the antagonist of all the gods. But this does not mean that all materialist-inclined philosophers, including the founders of materialism, were outright and conscious atheists. Far from it. Atheism is contained in materialism as the fruit is potential in the seed. It is the logical outcome, the necessary conclusion of materialist thought. Total rejection of the gods, however, does not occur all at once. The materialists approached this point gingerly and gradually and did not drive through to the end until several thousand years later.

The older materialists did not explicitly deny the existence of the gods; they offered explanations of the world which rendered divine powers more and more unnecessary and useless. They relegated the gods to the background and to the sidelines, deposing them from sovereignty and depriving them of their principal powers and functions.

This process in philosophy was analogous to what happened in politics in the struggle against the equally ancient and strongly established institution of the monarchy. The anti-monarchist forces in the Western world did not at first assault kingship in its central citadel but strove rather to restrict it by abridging absolute rule, setting up other countervailing powers, and acquiring a constitution. Republican movements, which aspired to do away in theory and practice with monarchy as such, appeared only at the climax of protracted conflicts. These stages were passed through not only in Greece but also in our own country's early history.

It was the same with the sovereignty of the gods in the realms of thought and their representatives in society. The first efforts of the materialists cut down the powers of the gods and assigned their functions to material processes and forces. They sapped the supports of divinity without demolishing it.

Xenophanes of Colophon (570-470), one of the twelve Ionian cities, began the undermining by his radical criticism of the prevailing polytheism. He carried forward the scientific work of the Milesians and was very likely the earliest geologist and paleontologist. From the fossil remains of shells, fishes, and marine animals found in Syracuse, Paros and Malta he deduced that these deposits in the earth had once been mixed with the sea. He also viewed the rainbow as a natural phenomenon in a way that clashed outright with the traditional myth. "She that they call Iris, is a cloud likewise, purple, scarlet and green to behold," he said.

Xenophanes attacked the legends of the gods set forth by the poets Homer and Hesiod and undertook to explain how the gods themselves had been fabricated by human heads and hands. He satirized the popular conceptions of the gods, declaring that men had created them in their own images. That was why there were so many different deities, each the product of different nations and needs.

The gods were given clothes, bodies, a voice and special functions like the people who conceived them, he said. Ethiopian gods were black and snub-nosed; Thracian gods have red hair and green eyes. If oxen, lions and horses had hands like men and could draw, they would doubtless make gods in their own shape. This was an anticipation of Feuerbach's theory that religion arises out of man's unconscious objectification and idolization of his own nature.

In place of the more primitive notion of many gods with blatant human characteristics, Xenophanes put forward the conception of one god who was elevated far above ordinary humans and given the entire universe for his domain. His view that "God is one and all" was monotheistic and even pantheistic. He retained the basic concept but reduced the authority and awesomeness of the gods, stripping them of mystery and bringing them closer to earth by exposing their man-made features.

Freethinking about the gods became widespread in Athens toward the close of the 5th Century B.C. The teachings of the naturalists and Sophists helped weaken belief in the old religion. The first unmistakable statement of an atheistic outlook appeared in the age of Socrates in a fragmentary passage from the satyric drama *Sisyphus*, which exposed religion as a cunning fraud imposed on men to maintain law and order in society.

However, such utterances were uncommon. Although certain Greek and Roman writers testify to the presence of atheists around them, unalloyed atheism was extremely rare in antiquity. Most of the philosophers took up intermediate positions between whole-hearted affirmations of the gods and skepticism about their attributes and existence. None of them draw their condemnations of the popular faith to its ultimate conclusion that the gods are a fabrication of the human imagination without objective reality.

Even though some were accused of godlessness because of their criticisms of the prevailing polytheism, none of the noted thinkers of Greece or Rome can be accounted an avowed atheist. Epicurus and Lucretius, whom we shall meet later, were genuine materialists and outspoken enemies of official religion—and yet they taught that gods existed. They only denied that the gods interfered with the operations of the universe or concerned themselves with human affairs. They retired the gods from office but did not assassinate or abolish them.

This ambiguous attitude toward divinity persisted among the leading materialist thinkers until quite recent times. It was not until the 18th Century that materialism became explicitly atheistic and God's existence was openly denied. Timidity on this sensitive point was especially marked in 18th Century England and North America where all the materialists stopped short of repudiating divine existence.

The decisive break was made by the French materialists who heralded the oncoming French Revolution. The last compromise, confusion and equivocation was thrown off by Baron Von Holbach in his *System of Nature* published in 1770 which categorically disclaimed belief in the existence of God. Yet even Holbach reverted to the standpoint of the Milesian pioneers by saying that the only notion of God which is not absurd is that which identified Him with the moving power in nature. However, Holbach and Diderot reserved atheism for scholars and scientists, the enlightened elite; it was presumably beyond the comprehension of the inescapably ignorant and superstitious masses, "much too good for the common people."

This course of development demonstrates that the relationship between materialism and atheism has been a dialectical one. Materialism is potentially, inherently atheistic; atheism is the appropriate form of its conception of the universe, the perfected result in which its essential content is most clearly and fully defined. But the first manifestations of materialism are incompletely atheistic. It required an extended and complex historical elaboration before materialism reached the crowning consciousness that both reality and its own premises were totally incompatible with religion.

⊡ Heroes of Thought

WHATEVER ARCHAIC AND
erroneous ideas they retained, the Milesians were the
first to interpret nature in its own terms instead of in
a supernatural manner. This feat is sometimes ac-
claimed as a "miracle." But it must have had substantial causes.

What impelled and enabled these "wise men" to con-
ceive the universe as a self-originating, self-determin-
ing, self-regulating process? We have almost no reliable
biographical information which could cast light on
the specific problems and immediate motives which
stimulated them to regard the physical cosmos as an
independent object, an external reality developing in
accord with its own laws. We must remain content with
some general observations.

The technological innovations and economic changes
in Aegean civilization which gave the residents of the
Ionian city-states greater control over their material
surroundings likewise provided the starting point
for their qualitatively different insight into the "nature
of nature." Farrington has pointed out in *Greek Science* how Thales may have drawn his theory of the
making of the universe from the silting up of the deltas which he could have noted in his travels to Egypt
or in the Ionian harbors. Anaximander interpreted
the processes of nature in accord with the observations
and reflections remindful of the potter's yard, the

113

smelter and the kitchen. Anaximenes may well have taken the idea of condensation upon which his cosmology was built from the industrial process of felting woven materials by pressure. Heraclitus may have selected fire as his first principle because it was the agency of change among craftsmen in the kitchen and the smithy as well as on earth and in the heavens.

"The Milesians," Farrington concludes, "were not simply observers of nature. They were observers of nature whose eyes had been quickened, whose attention directed, and whose selection of phenomena to be observed had been conditioned by familiarity with a certain range of techniques. The novelty of their modes of thought is only negatively explained by their rejection of mystical and supernatural intervention. It is its positive content that is decisive. Its positive content is drawn from the techniques of the age" —(pp. 36-37).

However, the "positive content," as well as the rational dialectical form, of their speculations did not come straightway from the transformations in their dealings with external reality through the improved technology. The raw materials of their materialist ideas were more immediately formed by the changes in their relations with one another brought about by the extension of the social division of labor, production for the market and money relations.

It is often remarked that the habit of keen and accurate observation of the world around them was a Greek characteristic. The Milesians exhibited this skill not only in their scientific investigations but also in the articles of daily use and the commodities they manufactured for export. It can be seen in the realistic concern for careful detail with which their potters traced the delicacy of a leaf, the coils of a tendril or the supple movement of a cat.

The Milesians did not explore nature for its own sake. They most energetically and successfully studied those processes and objects of nature which were involved in their occupations and preoccupations. The central place taken by meteorology in their inquiries undeniably arose not merely from their coastal location but from their far-reaching maritime, commercial and colonizing activities. They focussed attention—from meteorology to metallurgy—upon those aspects of their surroundings which were most vital to the purposes of production and exchange.

Consider the well-known statement by Heraclitus: "All things are exchanged for fire, and fire for all things, just as goods for gold and gold for goods." This was not just a casual comparison. It shows how monetary transactions on a broad scale guided abstract thought, stimulated the capacities for generalization and the habit of noting regularities amidst varied phenomena. Heraclitus took this mode of thought generated by the commercialized economy and applied it to the phenomena of nature. He not only pictured but interpreted the processes of universal development by means of commercial categories. Fire was the medium through which all other elements were circulated and transformed, just as money was the means for the circulation of commodities. Here the concepts of philosophy transparently reproduced economic realities.

The political, legal and ethical relations and ideas issuing from the democratic movement contributed directly to the formation of the new viewpoint. Philosophy was born at the same time as the democratic state in the maritime trading centers. One was an ideological, the other a political product of the periodic wars and class wars involving the merchants and shipowners, sailors, iron-workers, wool-workers, carpet-makers, dyers, artificers of weapons and urbanized owners of vineyards and corn-lands. These convulsive conflicts gave sharp point to the observations of Heraclitus and others that everything was in flux and that change was brought about by the tension and unbalancing of opposing forces in which the ruler of today is the outcast of tomorrow, the good and the bad change places, and strife is the master of existence.

This was the period in Greek history when custom was being supplanted by codification of the laws. Such critical scrutiny of the old order resulting in the rule of society by written law induced the most thoughtful investigators in turn to seek for laws governing the occurrence and recurrences of events in nature and for the "justice" which necessarily regulates the cosmos. Thus Heraclitus says: "As it advances, fire will judge and convict all things."

The broader vistas of time and space disclosed to the Ionians by their travels stretched the boundaries of human history and the known world, helped relegate the gods to the background, and bring man and his works into greater prominence.

The expansion of their interests which broke through

the limitations of the past in politics, culture, and general theory were all bound up with the unprecedented expansion and diversity of their urban life. The main lines of their thought were directed by the deep-going innovations in their social setup, the demands of their commercial activities and the categories of their commodity-conditioned class culture.

In their infancy science and philosophy were almost exclusively leisure class pursuits. The progenitors of science in Mesopotamia and Egypt, star-gazers, calendar-makers, geometricians, numerologists, had been associated with the priesthoods. The naturalists of Miletus who were the first genuine scientists likewise belonged to the ruling classes of their day. Their wealth gave them the means, the time and the freedom to busy their intelligences with problems in the field of knowledge going beyond the narrow and immediate aims of everyday concern, even though these were essentially charted out by the requirements of commercial enterprise in their communities.

These learned men carried on their intellectual investigations apart from the manual labor of the plebeian orders and the slaves. However, the separation of theory from practice, inherent in any class society, was far less pronounced among the Milesian naturalists than it was to become two centuries later among the classical idealists of Athens.

There are heroes of thought as well as heroes of action in history. These are the first to grasp the essence of new developments, penetrate deeper into reality, formulate their discoveries in clear and fruitful concepts—and then fight for their adoption against outworn ideas and modes of thought. We shall meet with a number of such heroes in this review of the history of materialism.

The Milesian naturalists were such pathfinders in the field of philosophy. They are the first occupants in its hall of fame. They made a leap in the evolution of thought so audacious as to create an entirely new epoch.

Breasted, one of the founders of American archaeology and historian of early civilization, has paid them this merited tribute: "They entered upon a new world, which we call science and philosophy—a world which never dawned upon the greatest minds of the early East. This step, taken by Thales and the great men of the Ionian cities, remains and will forever remain the greatest achievement of the human intellect—an achievement to call forth the reverence and admiration of all time."—*The Conquest of Civilization* (pp. 317-318).

VIII. The Early Atomists

IN HIS WELCOMING ADDRESS to the delegates at the International Conference on the Peaceful Uses of Atomic Power at Geneva in August 1955, the Conference President and Chairman of the Indian Atomic Energy Commission, Dr. H. J. Bhabha, divided the history of civilization into three epochs according to their energy sources.

In the first period of the early civilizations in the Valley of the Euphrates, the Indus and the Nile, all the energy for doing work: tilling the ground, drawing water, carrying loads and for locomotion was supplied by either human or animal muscles. Molecular sources of energy, such as the chemical combustion involved in burning wood, were used only to a limited extent for cooking, heating and smelting. These restricted sources of power could not maintain mankind at more than a bare subsistence level.

This primitive energy pattern remained essentially

unchanged until the scientific and technical advances
from the 17th to the 19th Centuries enabled men to
make increasing use of chemical energy, especially
through the consumption of fossil fuels, coal and oil.
These sources of power made possible the industrial
revolution that initiated the second great epoch of
human history. Today 80 percent of the enormous
consumption of energy in the world is provided by
the combustion of coal, oil and gas, 15 percent by
burning wood and agricultural waste, 1-1/2 percent
by hydroelectric power and only about 1 percent by
muscular energy.

Now that the energy in the atom has been tapped,
entirely new and apparently inexhaustible power resources have been opened up for the use of mankind.
Dr. Bhabha rightly remarked: "The acquisition by
man of the knowledge of how to release and use
atomic energy must be recognized as the third great
epoch in human history." Atomic energy is far more
plentiful and concentrated than muscular or molecular
energy. We stand today on the threshold of this new
era.

Miletus on the shores of Asia Minor and Abdera in
Thrace where Leucippus and Democritus, the creators
of Greek Atomism, flourished in the 5th Century, B.C.,
are far removed in space and in time from Alamo-
gordo, New Mexico, and Hiroshima, Japan, where
the first atom bombs catapulted mankind into the
Atomic Age in 1945. Yet, although separated by
almost 2,500 years, there is a definite and discernible
link between them.

That connection is primarily an ideological and

methodological one. For it was from these 5th Century Greek thinkers that the original conception of the inner structure of the material world as atomic, and the very term itself, has come. This does not mean that the experiments of the 20th Century scientists have been derived in a straight line of descent from the speculations of the Greek Atomists. History does not proceed so simply and directly; the conditions and causes of such epoch-making developments are much more complex and their course more circuitous.

A vast variety of historical circumstances, rooted in the first organization of class society and culminating in its last form, had to interpose themselves between the enunciation of the first atomic hypothesis and the dawning of the Atomic Age. To select but one factor, the development of the techniques of metallurgy was no less necessary for the construction of atom bombs and reactors than the elaboration of correct theories of matter. The development of metallurgy in turn depended largely upon the evolution of industry and warfare which was determined in its main lines by the changing needs of class society from the beginnings of slavery to the climax of capitalism.

But this does not detract from the fact that the current of thought about the structure of the material world set in motion by the Greek Atomists was one of the indispensable historical preconditions for the achievements of the present day atomic scientists. As their forerunners in the field of ideology and method, the Greek Atomists deserve a very high place in the history of science and human thought.

However they have rarely been accorded proper

recognition. In antiquity, although their personal attainments were honored, the methods and conclusions of the founders of Atomism were by and large low-rated. Plato does not even mention the ideas of the Atomists in his writings and is reputed to have said he would like to burn all the works of Democritus. The Atomists were jeered at by the Aristotelian Academy. This traditional disparagement has, with notable exceptions, persisted up to our own day.

We shall see later why the Atomists were so scorned in antiquity. But first we must find out what they did and why they were so important in the evolution of Greek philosophy and the history of materialism.

▣ Greek Atomism and Science

THE ATOMISTS WERE THE second outstanding school of materialist philosophy in Greece; the Milesian naturalists were the first. There are differences of opinion among scholars regarding the precise affinity between the two schools. But, from the standpoint of the formation of the materialist philosophy, it is plain that the Atomists carried forward the Milesian investigations of nature and speculations about its processes in the light of the subsequent criticisms and contributions of the Greek philosophers and the intervening evolution of Greek society. Gomperez, a German authority on Greek thought, correctly characterized Atomism as "the ripe fruit on the tree of the old Ionic doctrine of matter which had been tended by the Ionian physiologists."—*Greek Thinkers* (Vol. I, p. 323).

The Atomists gave a more consistent and extensive development to the ideas and methods of the pioneer materialists. Anaximenes, for example, had explained that the differences of things were due to the differences in their densities brought about by rarefaction and condensation. But the processes of rarefaction and condensation cannot be clearly pictured except on the assumption that indiscernible particles are coming closer together or going further apart in space. This deeper insight into the hidden operations of material processes was supplied by the Atomists.

We have already explained why the first form of philosophy originated among the Milesians necessarily had to be materialistic in intention and direction. Now it has to be pointed out that along with the production of philosophy and materialism, a third cultural acquisition was brought into being. This was science as a rational method of dealing with reality, interpreting its processes in a systematic way and thereby promoting man's insight and control over nature. This triple birth of philosophy, materialism and science dates from the Milesians.

Before their time mankind had gathered many kinds of knowledge about the parts of the world and their movements which had been incorporated into the techniques of ancient society and formulated in its dominant notions. These provided the raw materials for the fabrication of the various sciences. The Greeks were the first to take this disorderly empirical information derived from everyday practice and material production and transform it into theoretically based branches of science, each having a special method of its own arising from a rational system of conception and investigation.

They did not do this in all fields. The Greeks lagged behind in the theoretical development of chemistry, for example. The empirical origins of chemistry go back as far as the metal workers and expert goldsmiths of 3000 B.C. in Egypt. The Egyptians were so skilled in the arts of metallurgy, enameling, glass-tinting, and the extraction of oils from plants and dyeing that the country became famed as the motherland of chemistry. The very term is taken from the

Arabian name for Egypt, Khem, the country of black soil.

But neither the Egyptians nor their successors, the Greeks, succeeded in extracting a sound body of chemical theory from the crafts of the potter, the dyer or the smith. In fact, chemistry had to pass through the incubator of alchemy and wait until the expression of modern atomic theory in the latter part of the 18th and the beginning of the 19th Centuries before it acquired a genuine scientific foundation.

However, the Greeks did lay the basis for scientific theory in a remarkable number of branches of knowledge: in mathematics, in physics, in biology, medicine, history, politics, logic and several other departments of the natural, social and mental sciences.

In antiquity no distinction was drawn between philosophy and science. The two were so intermingled that they were not, and cannot be, separated. The first philosophers were likewise the earliest scientists. The many-sided Thales was an astronomer, geometrician and engineer as well as a philosopher, businessman and statesman. The same holds true for many of the other leading figures in Greek philosophy of all tendencies.

Except in medicine, the specialization, compartmentalization and professionalism now current among scientists, as well as the division and even antagonism between the philosophers and scientists, was largely absent in Graeco-Roman times. The sciences grew up under the shelter and superintendence of philosophy until in the bourgeois era they parted from their mother and nurse and set up housekeeping on their own account.

One of the main reasons for this subsequent alien-
ation of the sciences from philosophy was the fact
that after antiquity religion and its attendant idealist
philosophy came into more and more open and direct opposition to the methods and results of the natural sciences and thwarted their further growth. This
does not mean that idealists have always had an
adverse influence on the progress of the sciences. Although the basic premises and conclusions of idealism
are wholly unscientific, this hasn't prevented the classical idealist philosophers from Socrates to Hegel
from making significant contributions to one or
another of the sciences.

The relation between science and materialism, however, has had a more consistent and organic character. Materialism was born together with the first successful essays in scientific method and the two have
remained intimate associates ever since. The interaction
between them has operated both ways. The development
of the sciences has promoted the progress of materialism while the methods and ideas of materialism
have helped the sciences to move ahead.

The article on "Materialism" in *The Encyclopedia
of Religion and Ethics* contains pertinent testimony
to this historical symbiosis of materialism and science.
"The chief outbursts of materialistic metaphysic have
coincided," it says, "with occasions of renewed interest
in, or remarkable progress of physical science. The
emergence of this tendency to regard the world as
fundamentally material, at successive epochs in the
history of thought, is evidence that materialism strongly
commends itself to many minds, especially to those

whose studies chiefly lie in the sphere of the physical sciences." This observation is all the more significant because its author, F. R. Tennant, an English don, was a philosophical and religious opponent of materialism.

The natural partnership of the two has historically expressed itself in both negative and positive ways. The stagnation of the sciences coupled with the decay of Western society after the 2nd Century A.D. led to the discouragement and the prolonged dispossesion of materialist thought in Europe; on the other hand the upsurge of the sciences in the 15th and 16th Centuries stimulated the revival of materialist ideas. From antiquity to the present day the two have marched hand in hand. It is only the materialist trend in philosophy which can be considered thoroughly scientific, that is, rooted in a true appraisal of the nature of reality and its processes of development.

Science is just as dependent upon materialism which has provided it with a correct theoretical foundation and procedure as materialism is dependent upon the sciences which give it acquisitions of knowledge which have been verified in practice. Each decisive forward step in society's knowledge of its environment and mastery over nature has enriched the content and elevated the form of the materialist outlook. The materialist schools for their part have not only sought to keep pace with the discoveries and developments of the sciences but have even at times anticipated and prepared the way for them.

On the other hand, the philosophy of materialism could not leap very much ahead of the specific stage of scientific development and has shared and reflected the deficiencies of the sciences.

This interplay between the sciences and materialism is most conspicuous in antiquity among the Atomists. They not only continued the speculations of the Milesians and heralded the ideas of modern chemistry and the Atomic Age. The theories of Leucippus, Democritus, Epicurus and Lucretius and their fellow thinkers on the nature of matter, the origins and operations of the universe, and the history of society and civilization were the mountain peaks of scientific thought in the ancient world.

As Farrington has emphasized in his review of *Greek Science:* "The true glory of the atomism of Democritus is that it answered better than any current theory the problems of his own day. It is the culmination in antiquity of the movement of rational speculation on the nature of the universe begun by Thales. Its factual basis consists in the observation of technical and natural processes by the unaided senses, together with a few experimental demonstrations of the kind we have described. Its theoretical merit is to have reduced these results to a greater logical coherence than any other ancient system."

▣ The Philosophical Background of Atomism

FROM ITS BIRTH TO ITS extinction at the close of the 2nd Century A.D. the history of the Atomist school stretches over seven centuries. We shall deal only with the main lines of its development during that period.

The first two illustrious names associated with the Atomic school are Leucippus and Democritus. They flourished in the 5th Century B.C. and were likewise natives of Ionia. Leucippus was born in Miletus; his co-thinker Democritus came from the prosperous city of Abdera.

The earliest Greek analyzers of nature traced the origins of things back to four elements: fire, earth, water and air and singled out one of these as the substantial source of the rest. This "elementary" conception of the fundamental stuff of matter and the beginnings of its diverse manifestations not only dominated the thought of the ancient world but persisted until modern times. Recognition of the existence of many more basic chemical components is relatively recent. As late as 1764 Voltaire wrote in his famous *Philosophical Dictionary* that only the four traditional elements need be reckoned. These were displaced from chemical science only after Lavoisier demonstrated the existence of oxygen in the late 18th Century and inaugurated the new sequence and type of basic elements. Now almost a hundred natural elements — and some man-made ones — make up the chemical table.

The four elements, fire, earth, water and air, were all physically observable things. But when they were used to explain all the varied phenomena of the world, they assumed an increasingly abstract and generalized character. These four states of matter not only passed over into one another but were the substantial realities of all other manifestations of matter. Fire in the form of earth, or bone or sight was a quite different entity, at least in appearance and to the senses, than fire as flame.

How could one and the same thing appear to be, or become, so many other things? These and similar questions arising from the very development of the Milesian cosmology set a series of new problems before the Greek philosophers for solution. These problems were formulated in the following terms. What is the relation between the one and the many, the permanent and the changing, identity and difference, being and non-being? And how do we know what these are? Does a knowledge of reality and the truth come through the reason or the senses?

This new trend in thought coincided with a shift in the center of Greek philosophical activity from one sector of Greek culture to another, from Asia Minor to the Greek colonies in Sicily and Southern Italy. This shift is personified in Pythagoras, the founder of the Pythagorean community, who at the age of 40, about 530 B.C., had to flee from the Persian conquest of his native Ionia and settle in Croton in Southern Italy.

Under the influence of mathematics and religion, the thought of the Pythagoreans took a different turn from that of the Milesians. They did not describe the universe in terms of the operations of specific material elements and physical processes. They were the first to recognize the important role numbers could play in the knowledge of things and they went so far as to make numbers the fundamental substance of the universe. For them physics was equated with mathematics.

This general idea, taken by itself, has proved immensely fruitful in the history of science. However, in the excitement of their discovery that mathematical relations were discernible all about them, the Pythagoreans enormously exaggerated the power and applicability of numbers. They saw an identity between reality and mathematics where there was no more than an interdependence and correspondence.

This identification of numbers with things was made easy for the Pythagoreans because they represented numbers in figurative form, like the dots in dominoes. Moreover, their arithmetic was tightly tied to their geometry. The Pythagoreans called a point *one*, a line *two*, a surface *three*, and a solid *four* and constructed their conception of the world out of these number-dimensions.

The Pythagoreans took still another important step in their thinking. They insisted that these mathematical relations which made up the universe could be truly perceived and understood only through the reasoning processes. Their theory of the universe and of knowledge exalted logical procedures and the results of abstract thought far above the study of the physical processes and states, like rarefaction, condensation, and tension, and the practical techniques and direct sensuous observation which were in the foreground of Ionian thought.

Parmenides of Elea, the founder of another Italian school, pushed this line of abstract thought and exaltation of pure reason to its ultimate conclusion. The Greek thinkers had already arrived at three fundamental general ideas in analyzing the nature of reality. These were the categories of being, not-being and becoming. Parmenides sought to clarify the content and the interrelation of these three aspects of reality.

The axis of his inquiry was the character of being and the path of knowing it. Heraclitus had declared that everything changes. This sense of the evanescent nature of things in which everything is turned topsy-turvy and becomes something very different from what it once was haunted the minds and imaginations of the Greeks who lived in a turbulent and changing society. This was explicitly expressed by Herodotus, the first historian, who lived about the same time. He observed: "For many states that were once great have become small, and those that were great in my time were small formerly."

Socrates said: "Summon the philosophers, only excepting Parmenides, and summon the poets with them—they all say that nothing is, for all things are constantly becoming." Except Parmenides. He declared that everything is and that nothing is not—and that never the twain could meet. What induced him to deny so categorically what others affirmed?

What arguments did he use to justify his opposing position?

Parmenides was bothered by the contradictory nature of things evidenced in their changes and the application of the logical principle of contradiction to the condition of change. The principle of contradiction, formally understood and statically applied, says that everything must either be one thing or another; it cannot be both at one and the same time. A choice must be made between them. Parmenides took this principle with absolute seriousness and it stood in his way like a stumbling block.

The very essence of change and becoming is that it expresses the transition from what is to what is not and from what is not to what is. But Parmenides could not reconcile the coexistence of what is with what is not. Everything, he reasoned, either is or it is not. What is, is—and what is not has no reality whatsoever. This is certainly so according to a strict application of the formal rule of contradiction.

Therefore what *is* exists in full actuality and cannot at any time or in any way be contaminated by its excluded opposite, not-being. If this be so, he concluded, all change, motion and show of variety is unreal, an illusion of the senses, and only being is truly real.

Parmenides believed that the road of logical thought alone led to perfect truth. So he clung firmly to the law of contradiction and did not shrink from the logical consequences of its rigid application. He could not admit that a thing, in fact every thing, could both be and not be at one and the same time. The law of contradiction, as he conceived, understood and invoked it, forbade such a conclusion. But change, in which a thing passes from what it is to what it is not, cannot be accounted for except by acknowledging the co-presence of being and not-being and their transformation into each other through the process of becoming.

Parmenides solved the problem by denying the reality of change, becoming and not-being. He regarded these states as errors of opinions, confusions and illusions of the senses, and asserted that unchangeable, immovable, uniform being alone was real and truly known.

Parmenides thereby brought forward two viewpoints which exercised considerable influence on the subsequent course of Greek thought. One was his insistence that purely logical thought was the sole road to truth and knowledge of reality. This involved the disparagement of sense impressions and practical activities.

The other was his equating of reality with what was perfect, unchangeable, ungenerated. The Eleatic school helped stamp this combination upon Greek thought; it will be found not only at the basis of classical idealism but also in the Atomist's conception of the basic unit of being.

The next great thinker among the Western Greeks, Empedocles of Agrigentum in Sicily, defended the validity of the evidence of the senses attacked and rejected by the Pythagoreans and the Eleatics. But he advised and practiced a more cautious and critical use of the testimony provided by sense-perception.

By experiment with the water clock he was the first to demonstrate that air, although invisible, has body, could occupy space, and exert power. He showed the distinction between air and empty space.

The theoretical importance of this discovery lay in the experimental proof that matter could exist in a very refined state and produce effects even though it was too small and subtle to be seen or observed directly by the senses.

Anaxagoras, a philosopher of the Ionian school who was brought to Athens by Pericles in the middle of the 5th Century, devised further experiments which showed that there were physical processes which took place below the level or beyond the range of direct perception. He took two vessels, one containing a white liquid and the other a black, and then transferred the liquid from one into the other drop by drop. Although physically there must be a change of color with each drop, this change is not discernible until several drops have been mingled.

From these experiments Anaxagoras drew the conclusion that the senses are not exact judges of real conditions, although their perceptions are not wholly misleading. The evidence of sense-perception must be used in order to arrive at the truth: to grasp the invisible, as in a gradual change in color, we must rely on the visible.

In his physical theory Anaxagoras went beyond Empedocles in another respect. Empedocles adhered to the four elements as his first principles. Anaxagoras presented a more complex picture of the nature of matter. He stated that the first principles, which he called "seeds," were infinite in number and variety and every one of these infinitely small particles, which are indestructible and unchanging, contained within itself the qualities of everything else.

These were some of the principal developments in the field of philosophy after the Milesians which formed the ideological background out of which the specific theories of the Atomists emerged.

IX. The Views of the Atomists

WHAT WERE THE TEACHINGS of the Atomists, and especially what were their views on the constitution of matter?

The theories of the Atomists aimed to take into account the contributions and criticisms of their philosophical predecessors and to provide solutions for the problems they had raised or difficulties they had met. The Milesians had sought to discover the substantial source of all things in one of the four elements or in Anaximander's unlimited stock of matter but could not satisfactorily explain the totality of things by means of a single element.

Heraclitus had defended absolute becoming and universal change in all things by the unity, tension and strife of their opposites and stated that their stability was transitory. The logic of the Eleatics on the other hand had concluded that being alone was real; all things were essentially fixed and motionless; change was an illusion of the senses.

Empedocles and Anaxagoras had tried to rescue the reality of change, motion and the varied appearances of things from the excommunication pronounced by the Eleatics in three ways. They conceived the first principles as many and even as infinite in number and variety. They attributed the creation and destruction of things to the coming together and separation of these elements. Finally they showed that the human understanding, by inference based on observation, could discover processes in nature that were real and effective though not directly and completely perceptible to the senses.

Taking off from these thoughts and controversies, the co-creators of Atomism, Leucippus and Democritus, postulated two kinds of ultimate existence. These were the full and the empty, the something and the nothing, the atom and the void. One was equivalent to being; the other to not-being. Thus, in opposition to the Eleatics, the Atomists asserted the real existence of not-being in the form of the void or empty space and derived change and variety from the interaction between the atom and the void.

Aristotle's successor as head of the Academy in Athens, Theophrastus, wrote of Leucippus: "He assumed innumerable and ever-moving elements, namely, the atoms. And he made their forms infinite in number, since there is no reason why they should be one kind rather than another, and because he saw there was unceasing becoming and change in things.

He held, further, that *what is* is no more real than *what is not,* and both are alike causes of the things that come into being: for he laid down that the substance of the atoms was compact and full, and he called them *what is,* while they moved in the void which he called *what is not,* but affirmed to be just as real as *what is.*"

Thus, by their specific union of *what is* with *what is not,* the Atomists reconciled the contradictory positions of Heraclitus that everything flowed and of Parmenides that nothing changed. The coupling of the atoms with the void explained both permanence and change, motion and rest, identity and difference. Neither changed in themselves but their incessant interactions gave rise to all the changes, combinations and differences of things in the universe.

The atom of Leucippus and Democritus was compounded of characteristics borrowed from the basic ideas of their predecessors. It was similar to the single primary substance of the Milesians and to the notion of the Pythagoreans that numbers are constituents of things. The atom was uncreated and unchangeable like the one being of Parmenides yet plural in number and ever-involved in combinations like the four elements of Empedocles or the "seeds" of Anaxagoras.

Gross matter was composed of these granules or particles. The atoms were uncreated, solid and uniform in substance, unchangeable, and absolutely impenetrable. They formed one element of irreducible reality. "Atom" means what cannot be further cut, divided or separated.

The atoms differed intrinsically in size and shape; extrinsically in their position and arrangement in respect to one another. Some were hooked, others rough and smooth, angular and curved. They could be any size but were so extremely small as to escape observation by the senses. That is how the atom was pictured on its first appearance to mankind.

Of equal importance in the system of the Atomists was their conception of the void. It is necessary to place special emphasis upon this second factor because its significance is sometimes slighted. Yet the pair was inseparable in the minds of the Atomists; the void is no less essential to their theories than the atom. Together they generated the rest of the universe.

The notion of the void made motion theoretically explicable as well as sensibly apparent. The void in which the atoms moved and had their being was likewise uncreated and changeless, solid and uniform in nature, but it was completely featureless and wholly penetrable. The void was as passive and permeable as the atoms were restless and self-enclosed.

This concept of the vacuum has a history in philosophy and science as interesting and instructive as that of its companion, the atom. It was the prototype of the notions of infinite and empty space of the ancients, the extension of the Cartesians, the ether of the 19th Century physicists and the electro-magnetic field of the contemporary scientists. Today's physicists are still grappling with the difficulties involved in the relations between the electro-magnetic field and the smallest units of matter. It can be said without exaggeration that they have still to solve problems first posed when the Greeks distinguished the atom from the void.

How, according to the Atomists, was the cosmos formed? A swarm of atoms of differing shapes separated from the infinite mass, spread through empty space, collided by accident. They became entangled, eddied around in a circle. Like adhered to like; the light atoms flew outward and the rest stayed together. Out of this whirling conglomeration of atoms and the separation of its components into similars, not only our world and all its bodies but also an infinite number of other worlds were created and destroyed.

This cosmic process continues without end. Everything comes into existence and goes out of it through the collision, coagulation and dissolution of the atoms moving in the void. The different qualities and appearances of things are due to the differing combinations of their constituent atoms with their different shapes, sizes, positions and groupings. Just as there are different letters in the alphabet with different positions and different orders of arrangement, so the many atoms by their varied combinations compose the many different things in the universe.

In their theories the Atomists strove to satisfy both the evidence of their senses and the requirements of reason. Their assertion that every particular thing was made up of atoms went far beyond the immediate observations of the senses. It rested upon the inference that directly perceptible things and changes were caused by material elements and movements hidden from the senses under ordinary conditions. To account for observed phenomena they assumed that matter had a minute granular structure which was beyond the range of direct verification.

They believed that the atoms were actual bodies, materially existing realities, or as Democritus termed them, something as contrasted with empty space which was nothing. The audacity of their conviction that the atoms were not fictions can be gauged by the fact that the real existence of atoms was questioned by some foremost scientists right up to the beginning of the 20th Century. These positivists considered the atom a useful conceptual device for explaining certain molecular phenomena but doubted whether this convenient hypothesis designated any objective reality.

On these general grounds, Ernst Mach, one of the most influential theorists of natural science at the turn of the century and an exponent of the philosophy of empirio-criticism, explicitly denied that atoms really existed. Fifty years ago he repudiated what the atom bomb has dramatically demonstrated to ignorant backwoodsmen today. This is pointed out not to denigrate Mach, whose criticisms of certain theoretical assumptions of Newtonian physics influenced Einstein and others in the speculations leading to relativity and the discovery of atomic energy, but to underscore the penetrating theoretical vision of the Atomists. Their ideas were as daring as they were novel.

There was, to be sure, a colossal distance between the ideas of the Atomists on the structure of matter and the current practical uses of atomic power. It is the distance between a theoretical anticipation and a proof in deeds. Ideas are most indisputably verified when men can produce or destroy what they stand for.

*   *   *

The Atomists had many wrong notions about the universe. One was the misconception that larger bodies fall faster in empty space than smaller ones. Another was their belief that the fundamental physical elements were unchangeable and alike in substance. This view, which persisted for many centuries, has been disproved by modern science.

Dalton's experiments showed that the atoms of the elements were not alike; each had its characteristic weight. It has been demonstrated in our own century that even the weight of atoms of the same elements is variable (isotopes). We now know that instead of being incapable of alteration and division, atoms are highly mutable, fissionable and fusionable. Moreover, atoms can act and react upon one another not simply by mechanical pressure and collision but also in electrical and other ways.

All these subsequent developments in the knowledge of atomic properties do not invalidate the importance of the Atomists' discoveries in their own time and place. They gave as adequate and accurate a picture of the inner constitution of the natural world and the modes of its operation and evolution as was possible with the available information, techniques and ideas. Their specific errors were unavoidable under the prevailing rudimentary state of scientific knowledge and count for less than the admirable consistency of their cosmological conceptions in which all causes are uniformly physical and all consequences are materially determined.

The Atomists were strict determinists. The only surviving fragment of the teachings of Leucippus states: "Nothing happens without a reason, but all things occur for a reason, and of necessity." Nothing can be attributed to chance; everything has its cause from which it comes by necessity. Nothing is produced out of nothing; everything has its material antecedents upon which its existence depends.

These principles are indispensable conditions for the scientific investigation of nature. Scientific method is founded on the rejection of pure accident, teleology, final causes, or intelligent purpose as the explanation for natural events.

Black Power, a recent book by Richard Wright, contains an excellent illustration of the contrast between these two modes of interpreting natural phenomena. He tells about a flood in a sacred stream on the African Gold Coast which did considerable damage. The natives believed the flood expressed the anger of ancestral spirits who had to be propitiated and given their victims. They accordingly tried to prevent engineers sent in to investigate the natural causes of the torrent from devising practical measures to channel its flow and stop its destructive consequences.

In this case the ideas and practices of magic collided with the methods of science and ruled out the applications of engineering. The approach of the tribesmen was teleological. They looked upon this natural event as embodying the will and carrying out the purpose of ghostly powers instead of examining the real material conditions which produced it.

The Atomists resolutely rejected this animistic method. This was most plain in their basic conception of motion. The idealists sought some teleological reason for the existence of motion. To the Atomists motion had no first cause; it had always existed. Motion was an inherent feature of atoms in the void; any present movement was always conditioned and determined by a previous movement so that there was no need in their system for a prime mover or a divine interferer to keep things going.

Their thoroughgoing determinism was valid but one-sided. Accident is as fundamental a feature of reality as necessity. But Leucippus and Democritus alloted no place in their theories to chance. This was inconsistent because contingency was implied in their own account of the formation of things. The creation of the many worlds and their furniture was as much a matter of chance as of necessity. The cosmos was not alive, nor governed by any foresight, nor produced by any design. It had come together by the purely fortuitous concourse of atoms combining and separating in the void. This exclusion of accident from their scheme of things caused considerable difficulties for the Atomists which later members of the school tried, though unsuccessfully, to rectify.

*   *   *

Two important aspects of the philosophy of Democritus were subject to dispute even in antiquity. One concerned his views on matter and motion; the other his theory of knowledge.

Aristotle wrote that Leucippus and Democritus dismissed the origins of motion too lightly because, in his opinion, an intelligent force was needed to account for the initial motion of the cosmos. Later Simplicius and Cicero stated that the atoms had to be set into motion by virtue of some external impulsion.

The mechanical philosophers and physicists of the bourgeois epoch likewise assumed that Democritus shared their conception of matter as inherently inert. Boyle said that God "gave motion to matter" and Newton declared that "God in the beginning form'd matter in solid, massy, hard, impenetrable, movable particles . . ." In that case, the atoms, as the ultimate particles of matter, would have to be pushed from one place to another and from one state to another by mutual shock after the prime mover activated them. Lange declared that the Atomists were the first to set forth such "a strictly mechanical theory of the universe."

They all failed to grasp the main point of Democritus' position. He criticized Anaxagoras for introducing mind to set matter into motion and create order in the world. He regarded the movement of atoms in the void as an irreducible fact of existence for which there was no further explanation. This fundamental material process had neither beginning nor end; the movement of atoms in the void was infinite, everlasting, indestructible. Circulating at random in the illimitable emptiness, the products of their association and dissociation went through such complex forms of motion as birth, growth, attraction, repulsion, disintegration and destruction.

The fact that Democritus had pictured the atom as indivisible and unchangeable enabled Gassendi, Boyle, Newton and others to integrate his key concept into their schemes of physical and theological mechanism. But Democritus was not a mechanist in the modern sense; he was a naively dialectical materialist who viewed reality as a unified and unending flux of things coming into being, passing away, and giving rise to other things. Mathematics and physics were far too immature in Greek times to provide the basis for a scientific conception of the world on the model of the mechanical materialism of the 17th and 18th Centuries.

*   *   *

Some commentators declared that Democritus held skeptical or subjectivist views in regard to the evidence of the senses and the possibility of arriving at authentic knowledge about the external world through sense perception. He did make a distinction between two kinds of knowledge. "There are two forms of knowlege, the trueborn and the bastard," he wrote. "To the bastard belong all these: sight, hearing, smell, taste, touch. The trueborn is quite apart from these."

This might be taken to mean that he did not credit sense perception with any truth. Indeed, Lange aserted that "Democritus regarded the sense qualities, such as color, sound, heat, and so on, as mere deceptive appearances . . ." This misconstrues his position. Democritus did not intend to deprive the senses of their primary role in the process of knowledge. "All the senses," as Epicurus said, "are the heralds of truth." But the senses were not all-sufficient. They led to a deeper knowledge of reality through the use of reasoning which depended upon perception. Thought was not absolutely different from sensation but a further, more complex and subtle movement of the same images received from external sources and mirrored in the individual.

The two different modes of knowledge were based upon two different grades or levels of reality. What appeared on the surface of things, relayed by images passing through the air, was more or less accurately reflected by the senses. This knowledge of things was correct and reliable so far as it went. Aristotle stated that Democritus "judges as true what appears to us." But it was no more than opinion. "Truth is buried deep."

Genuine knowledge is of the atoms and the void which operate below the surface of appearances and generate them. These fundamental factors in nature are too minute to be directly perceived by the gross senses. Their existence and activity are inferred by the reason.

The atoms and the void are the sole "trueborn" object of scientific knowledge because they alone have unchanging existence. The diversified qualities of things perceived through the senses which result from their movements and combinations are true only by convention, Democritus says. This does not mean that sensory qualities have no objective reference or material causes, but rather that they are common to all people who experience these things.

The Atomists did not totally disqualify perception as the Eleatics did. They maintained that colors, tastes, sounds, smells and tactile qualities were *both* characteristics of objects and effects of their action upon the senses.

Democritus aspired to link up objective natural causes with sensory responses and sensation with the generalizing powers of the reason. The physician Galen wrote on this point: "After discrediting the appearance of things by saying: 'color is a convention, the sweet is a convention, the bitter is a convention, there are in reality only atoms and vacuum,' Democritus makes the senses speak as follows to reason: 'Poor reason, after depriving us of the means of proof, you want to beat us down. Your victory is also your defeat.' "

This ironic argument is directed against logicians like the Eleatics and Platonists who stigmatized sense qualities as illusory and thereby cut the ground from under their own feet. "Since the only evidence of any real existence you get comes from us," say the senses, "our downfall at your hands means your own over-throw."

The Atomists thereby sought to distinguish between the objective and subjective components in our sense perception of the external world and in the formation of our knowledge about it without making an abso-lute separation between them. This attempt was not viable. They restricted true knowledge to the simple, unchanging atoms and the void while knowledge of compound, ever-changing bodies was inferior. In this way Democritus denoted the difference between the outward show and inner reality of things, between appearance and essence. But he did not see clearly how the underlying material reality was connected with appearance and gave rise to it, nor explain how acquaintance with the qualities of things acquired through the senses gave valid knowledge of the atoms and the void.

This gulf between the atom and the void and sensible qualities, between permanent and ever-changing existences was not overcome by any materialist in antiquity and indeed remained one of the most vexing problems confronting the mechanical philosophers later on.

The psychology of the Atomists was one of their weakest points. They taught that the body was composed of coarse atoms; the soul or mind of fine, smooth, round atoms. The gods, who performed no essential functions in their system, were made of extra fine atoms. These crude ideas bear witness to their determination to bring all phenomena, from the heavenly bodies to life, sensation, mind and the gods, under the single all-embracing mode of a materialist explanation. But they equally testify to their inadequate knowledge of physiology and psychology.

*   *   *

The foregoing account has presented little more than the bare bones of the body of ideas produced by the first Atomists reconstructed from the surviving fragments of their works. Most of their writings have been lost. The scope of the interests and investigations which inspired and supported the ideas of the Atomist school can be judged from a list of their treatises compiled by later scholars of Alexandria. It covers such subjects as ethics; natural science (cosmology, astronomy, psychology and sense perception); logic (problems and criticisms of past theories); mathematics (geometry and numbers); music (rhythm and harmony, poetry and phraseology); technical works on medicine, agriculture, drawing and painting, and even military tactics; treatises on causes of celestial and meteorological, botanical, biological, geological phenomena; fire, sound, and many other things.

Although the main lines of their method of inquiry and analysis of nature were more correct than those of their rivals, the doctrines of the Atomists did not command a wide appeal in Greece or Rome. They did attract the allegiance of some of the finest minds, like Epicurus and Lucretius, but Atomism was not a popular or dominant school of thought.

Democritus had an encyclopedic knowledge and his qualities of intellect were on a par with those of Plato and Aristotle. Aristotle himself praised the originality and wisdom of Democritus in the highest terms, saying: "He seems to have reflected upon everything and in a clearly methodical manner."

Democritus was a learned mathematician whom Archimedes credited with being the first to formulate two important theorems on the properties of conic sections. One, that a cone is a third of a cylinder, and the other that a pyramid is a third of a prism with the same height and base. In astronomy he gave correct explanations of the nature of the Milky Way and the mountains of the moon. As a biologist, he carefully studied the internal organs of animals. He was likewise a theorist of colors and their mixtures.

Despite these achievements, Plato and Aristotle have been more highly esteemed and their teachings are better known than those of Democritus. This is not simply because much more of their writings have survived than those of the Atomists which have come down to us in bits and pieces.

The principal reasons for this disparity in prestige are to be found in their respective positions. The idealist views of Plato, Aristotle and their disciples fitted the needs of the slave aristocracy of Athens far better than the method and outlook of the Atomists— and they have more effectively aided the interests of ruling classes in the West ever since.

The history of philosophy has been recorded and taught by men who have been largely influenced by leisure-class psychology, religious and idealist conceptions. These scholars have therefore been inclined to see much more merit in the classical idealists than in the speculations of their materialist opponents. This has adversely affected the reputation of Democritus.

His work has not been properly valued because he was so uncompromising a materialist. Democritus did not endow nature with any conscious activity and rejected all the spurious supernatural, spiritual and final causes which tainted the speculations of the idealists. He set out to explain the formation and transformations of the universe, the origins of life, sensation, civilization, morals and thought—and even the existence of gods and demons—by purely natural causes based on the movements of atoms in empty space. He sought to do this in a unified manner all the way from the original fall of the atoms through space to the perceptions, thoughts and conduct of the people around him. This strict method with its consistent interconnection of physical, organic, social, historical and psychological processes and phenomena has been the prototype of all subsequent materialist systems of thought.

However, the original Atomists are slowly acquiring their rightful place in the front rank of contributors to intellectual progress. Sir Francis Bacon, the father of British materialism, saluted Democritus as the greatest of ancient philosophers. He was certainly among the foremost scientific minds of Graeco-Roman civilization.

In his book on the electron published in 1917, 2,300 years after the Atomists had first enunciated their principles, the American physicist and Nobel prize winner Millikan asserted: "These principles with a few modifications and omissions might almost pass muster today." Millikan was no friend of the materialist outlook in philosophy and yet, as a practicing scientist, he had to acknowledge the remarkable insight and farsight displayed by these eminent materialists of antiquity.

X. Greek Medicine and History

GREEK LIFE FROM THE 6TH to the 4th Centuries B.C. exemplified the point made in the foreword that materialist attitudes can be expressed in many other ways than philosophy. The same tendencies which promoted materialism at the summits of thought were likewise evidenced in Greek culture from its plastic arts to its playwriting.

Beginning with the latter part of the 6th Century, sculptors pulled away from the rigidity and solemnity of Egyptian and Oriental models to simulate the energy and spontaneity of the mobile human figure. Artistic craftsmen introduced fresh animation into stone, marble and bronze. The body ceased being symmetrical and rectangular and became curved; it bent and flexed in a variety of athletic postures; legs moved; hands opened up; drapery flowed in graceful folds; faces expressed intense emotions, individual character, different ages. However much it was idealized, the sensuous beauty of classical Greek sculpture reflected a delight in depicting human beings in action that was highly naturalistic.

The great tragic dramatists, Sophocles, Aeschylus and Euripides, reshaped the old myths into vehicles for presenting the religious, moral and intellectual predicaments of their time. They portrayed the conflicts between tradition and the new demands of Greek city life with such emotional force and poetic penetration that their audiences were stirred to reflect more deeply about the situations they staged. Euripides, the most radical, democratic and individualistic of the three, was indicted on a charge of impiety around 410 B.C. because of his irreverent treatment of the state religion. He described a soothsayer as "a man who speaks few truths and many lies." In another play, *Bellerophantes,* he cast doubt upon the very existence of the gods:

> *Doth some one say that there be gods above?*
> *There are not, no, there are not. Let no fool,*
> *Led by the false fable, thus deceive you.*

He maintained that the fortunes of man were not the work of supernatural beings but of natural causes or aimless chance. This rationalism went hand in hand with a sympathy for women and slaves and his condemnation of imperialist atrocities which Athens committed in the name of democracy.

It would be a diversion from our aim of tracing the main lines of philosophic thought to follow out such materialist trends elsewhere in Greek culture. However, two branches of achievement—the art of medicine and the writing of history—deserve special attention because of their more intimate affiliation with the advance of the materialist outlook in philosophy. Both acquired a scientific foundation as products of the powerful social and ideological movement which turned the minds of men from superstition toward naturalism and from despotism and oligarchy to democracy.

The practice of rational medicine first became an independent profession with its own methods of procedure precisely in the principal centers of philosophical, mathematical, scientific and political activity, first in Ionia, then Sicily and Southern Italy, finally in the chief commercial city-states of mainland Greece. These physicians were aligned with the philosophers, and most closely with the materialist schools, through their dissociation of the medical art from magic and religion.

According to the poet Hesiod:

Some 30.000 gods on earth we find
Subjects of Zeus. and guardians of mankind.

The ill-will of the gods toward men produced disease; their benevolence dispensed cures. The remedies for relief were therefore in the keeping of the priests. Besides prescribing special diets, exercises and folk recipes, these medicine men most of all relied upon incantations and exorcisms to drive out the evil spirits that made patients suffer.

The learned Greek physicians set aside the magical charms and rituals of the witch-doctors in order to bring the diseases of the body and the disturbances of the mind under careful observation and rational analysis. The new techniques and positive theories which these professionals advanced on the basis of their increased knowledge of the human organism took medicine a long step along the road that leads to our own day.

One of the earliest theorists of medicine was Alcmaeon of Croton, a center of Pythagorean influence in Southern Italy. He is credited with the discovery of the optic nerve, with speculations about the ear canals, and is said to have been the first to remove the eye by means of a surgical operation.

His most important discovery concerned the function of the brain as the seat of sensation and thought. Before Alcmaeon's time and even later, the heart was regarded as the common sensorium and the locus of thought. To the Romans, consciousness was not centered in the head but in the heart, the liver and the lungs. That is why their augurs consulted these organs for knowledge of the future. The current superstition that the wishbone of the turkey has prophetic virtues goes back to this belief that the seat of knowledge is located, not in the brain, but in the breast.

Alcmaeon, however, ascribed the function of thought to the brain to which bodily channels transmitted modifications produced in the sense organs by external stimuli. He was the first to practice dissection and to observe how every disturbance in the brain affects the sensibilities. He studied the organs and activities of sound, sight and taste. He placed the principle of life in the soul, which, like the stars, was immortal and moved forever in circular paths. He stated that animals as well as men possess sensation but only men possess intelligence which emerges from sensation.

In addition to these researches into embryology, anatomy, physiology and psychology, Alcmaeon put forward a general conception of health and sickness. Health is the result of the equilibrium and proportionate mixture of opposing qualities and forces: wet and dry, cold and hot, bitter and sweet. Sickness arises when one term of these contraries becomes supreme because the uncontrolled activity of any one of them tends to the elimination of its opposing principle. Health, therefore, consists in maintaining the balance of opposites. The search for the causes of illness should be directed to the search for the physical causes which upset this balance, such as a faulty diet or bad water.

Other more pronounced Pythagorean thinkers, notably Philolaus, developed a doctrine of medicine on the analogy of the world and its central fire. They taught that the principle of the human body seems to be the hot, and too much or too little temperature indirectly causes illnesses by acting upon the blood, humours and bile. Since the Pythagoreans attached special importance to the number four, both Philolus and Empedocles declared that there were four principal organs in the human body.

The most eminent school of medicine in antiquity was associated with Hippocrates of Cos, an Ionian island. The Hippocratic physicians of the 5th Century were more empirical-minded than their rivals and broke more drastically with the ideas and practices inherited from the barbarous past.

Just as Catholics today go to shrines like Lourdes for miracles of recovery through divine intervention, so credulous Greek pilgrims flocked to the sanctuaries of Aesculapius, the demi-god of healing, at Rhodes, Cos, Cnidos and Pergamos to seek cures through priestly witchcraft. Although they belonged to the clan or guild of Aesculapius, the men of the Hippocratic order counterposed to the magical mumbo-jumbo of the old wives and charlatans scientific procedures which aimed at finding out the material causes of the maladies affecting human beings.

They proceded from a resolute and conscious rejection of the divine or demonic origin of disease. The medicine men who believed that supernatural powers caused illness and death used various magical devices and incantations to expel them from the body, sometimes displaying a fetish supposed to contain the culpable evil spirit. Their treatment culminated in the elimination of the disturbing demon, or "crisis."

The Hippocratic men of medicine likewise looked for the crisis in the development of a sick person's condition when the substance which engendered the complaint was eliminated. But they discarded demonology entirely and interpreted the causes, the course of the disease and its crisis by purely natural factors.

Here are two citations from their collection of writings which illustrate their materialistic approach.

The Greeks called epilepsy "The Sacred Disease." The author of the Hippocratic treatise on this subject opened his discussion with the following blunt declaration: "I do not believe that the 'Sacred Disease' is any more divine or sacred than any other disease but, on the contrary, has specific characteristics and a definite cause. Nevertheless, because it is completely different from other diseases, it has been regarded as a divine visitation by those who, being only human, view it with ignorance and astonishment. This theory of divine origin, though supported by the difficulty of understanding the malady, is weakened by the simplicity of the cure . . .

"It is my opinion that those who first called this disease 'sacred' were the sort of people we now call witch-doctors, faith-healers, quacks and charlatans. These are exactly the people who pretend to be very pious and to be particularly wise. By invoking a divine element they were able to screen their own failure to give suitable treatment and so called this a 'sacred' malady to concel their ignorance of its nature."

Impotence was widespread among male Scythians who attributed the condition to God and worshipped the wretched victims, each dreading that the affliction would hit him. The Hippocratic commentator swept aside the fearful fancies of the popular religion. "In my opinion also these afflictions are divine, and all others likewise. There is none of them which is more divine or more human than another, but all are alike and all divine. Each of them has its own nature and none occurs except naturally." And the author goes on to give a natural theory of causation by attributing this sexual abnormality to the Scythian habits of life in the saddle.

One treatise on *Ancient Medicine* stands out as an incomparably clear statement of the principles of rational empiricism, i.e., of empirical skill raised to the higher level of a scientifically guided method. The author contended that clear knowledge about the nature of man could be obtained only from medicine. "It is this field of research which I claim for my own; viz., the nature of man and an accurate knowledge of causation in this field."

The art of healing, he said, did not come from the priest or the philosopher; it had the same humble ancestry as the techniques of the cook who prolonged human life by improving man's diet. The study of medicine, therefore, ought not to be based upon arbitrary presuppositions derived from philosophical speculation and still less upon recourse to the gods. "The nature of the body is the starting point of medical reasoning" and the foundation of its practice.

The Hippocratic physicians of Ionia criticized and condemned their rivals of the West for trying to deduce the rules of medical practice from *a priori* cosmological notions and abstract conceptions of the nature of things. "One must attend in medical practice not primarily to plausible theorizing, but to experience combined with reason. A true theory is a composite memory of things apprehended with sense perception. For the sense perception, coming first in experience and conveying to the intellect the things subjected to it, is clearly imaged, and the intellect, receiving these things many times, noting the occasion, the time and the manner, stores them up in itself and remembers. Now I approve of theorizing if it lays its foundation in incident, and deduces its conclusions in accordance with phenomena . . . but if it begins not from a clear impression, but from a plausible fiction, it often induces a grievous and troublesome condition. All who act so are lost in a blind alley."

These precepts indicate the empirical method adopted by the Hippocratic school. Their theory of knowledge based on case histories stood opposed to the more speculative schools of medicine which took a generalization from the field of natural philosophy as their starting point and tried to make that serve as the instrument of investigation into the physiological processes of concern to the physician. The Hippocratic specialists had a much more strict and concrete conception of scientific method. They first of all took into account the specific qualities of the phenomena in their field and continually checked their conclusions by further observations of the processes at work.

The Hippocratic physicians did not limit their consideration of health and illness to the isolated individual. They did not separate the mind from the body or divorce the body from its surroundings. They viewed man in relationship to his natural and social environment more consistently and profoundly than any other scientific tendency in antiquity. They took into systematic consideration the place the patient lived in, the food he ate, the kind of water he drank, and the air he breathed. One of their principal treatises was entitled: *Airs, Waters, Places.*

The Hippocratics were the first to try and correlate racial and national differences with both the natural and historical surroundings. They proposed to account for the peculiar habits and institutions of the

Persians, Scythians, Celts and other foreign nations by the influence of geographical factors. They went still further and brought under consideration the social and political circumstances affecting the patient, whether, for example, he was subjected to Greek freedom or Oriental despotism.

They fused empiricism and rationalism, accurate observations and reflective analysis, into a harmonious unity. "The examination of the body is a serious business, requiring good sight, good hearing, and sense of smell and touch and taste, and power of reasoning." All the information supplied by the senses and accumulated by experience had to be submitted to critical thought based upon rules drawn from similar cases.

The broad scope of the required medical examination is described in *Epidemics,* Book I: "The factors which enable us to distinguish between diseases are as follows: First we must consider the nature of man in general and of each individual and the characteristics of each disease. Then we must consider the patient, what food is given to him and who gives it—for this may make it easier for him to take or more difficult—the conditions of climate and locality both in general and in particular, the patient's customs, mode of life, pursuits and age. Then we must consider his speech, his mannerisms, his silences, his thoughts, his habits of sleep or wakefulness and his dreams, their nature and time. Next, we must note whether he plucks his hair, scratches or weeps. We must observe his paroxysms, his stools, urine, sputum and vomit. We look for any change in the state of the malady, how often such changes occur and their nature, and the particular change which induces death or a crisis. Observe, too, sweating, shivering, chill, cough, sneezing, hiccough, the kind of breathing, belching, wind, whether silent or noisy, hemorrhages and haemorrhoids. We must determine the significance of all these signs."

Having formed his diagnosis and prognosis and done all that he can, the physician must in the end rely upon nature to complete the cure. "Nature is the physician of diseases. It is nature herself who opens the way for her own action." The physician prescribes his therapy as the assistant of nature to help along the inherent regenerative capacities of the human organism.

"Life is short, science is long; opportunity is elusive, experiment is dangerous, judgment is difficult." These famous words summarize the spirit of the Hippocratic doctors. They combined deep concern for human welfare with a love of their art and a determination to improve it despite all obstacles. By their thirst for objective knowledge, the strictness of their investigations, their freedom from superstition, their sympathy for suffering fellow beings, their lack of discrimination between slaves and freemen, the members of the Hippocratic school were among the noblest exemplars of materialist humanism that the world has known.

*   *   *

The modes of materialist thinking originally applied by the philosophers to the physical world were soon extended to the history of mankind and later to the problems of knowledge. The Greeks were innovators in all three fields. They invented history and its companion sciences of cartography (map-making) and geography as well as physics, mathematics, psychology and logic.

Here, too, the Milesians sowed the seeds that the Athenians brought to fruition. The first writer who went beyond the mere recording of noteworthy events was Hecataeus of Miletus. Toward the end of the 6th Century he wrote two epoch-making works, one on history called the *Historiae,* or Inquiries, the other on geography, called the *Ges periodas,* or Circuit of the Earth, which described the known world from Sparta to India.

Up to his time the picture of the past held by the Greeks had been shaped by the epic poem of Homer. These were regarded as authentic accounts of ancient times in the same light as orthodox Jews and Christians do the Bible. Even Hecataeus accepted Homer as historical fact.

The more enlightened and literate classes of the prosperous commercial centers could no longer be satisfied with the legends of gods and heroes that entertained members of barbarian tribes or the celebrators of kingly reigns and deeds associated with despotic courts or temple cults. The far-travelling merchants and sailors and the free citizens who participated in the Assemblies, founded colonies, fought wars with Oriental powers and rival city-states, and witnessed democratic revolutions and oligarchic overturns demanded chroniclers on a par with their greater knowledge, more critical minds and broader outlooks.

The earliest historians set about to interpret human affairs along the same lines as those along which the philosophers explained the processes of nature. They wrote in prose instead of poetry and put aside ancient myths in a sustained effort to give the facts and find out the actual causes of events. Hecataeus emphasized this critical attitude in the opening sentence of the *Historiae:* "I write what I consider to be the truth; for the traditions of the Greeks seem to me many and various."

The works of Hecataeus were stimulated by the clashes between the Greeks and the neighboring Oriental kingdoms which tried to conquer them. The information which he compiled from various sources about the customs and background of Assyria, Medea and Persia, as well as Ionia and ancient Greece, considerably enlarged the historical horizon of his contemporaries.

Herodotus (484 ?—425 B.C.), who wrote in the next century, based his great work upon the model and materials supplied by Hecataeus. He narrated the relations between the Greeks and the Oriental powers from the accession of Croesus in Lydia around 560 B.C. to the capture of Sestos in 478 B.C. Within the framework of these struggles he ranged through time and space to tell the reader whatever he had seen or learned about the known world.

Herodotus deserves to be called the first ethnologist as well as "the father of history." His work is a treasure trove of information about the diverse cultures of antiquity from the civilizations of Greece, Persia, and Egypt to the customs of the barbarian tribes around them. Although skeptical of many legends, he did not wholly throw off credulity about ancient traditions or abandon belief in the gods' control over events.

Herodotus derived the theoretical framework for the biographical and historical events which he recounted from the conception of crime and punishment found in the Greek epic, drama and philosophy. The *hubris* of the aggressor, his excessive ambitions, provoked the *nemesis* of a corresponding retaliation. Thus, from the Trojan war to his own day, the Greeks and Orientals had alternately been encroaching on one another and then paying the penalty for this injustice. In this Heraclitean conflict of opposites he vindicated the role of the Greeks, and Athenian domination in particular, by their defense of freedom and democracy against Persian tyranny.

The increasingly rational and realistic approach to history introduced by Hecataeus and Herodotus was perfected by the master of Greek historians, Thucydides (*ca.* 471-399 B.C.). He set himself the task of recording the 27-year conflict between Athens and Sparta known as the Peloponnesian War (431-404 B.C.). He stated at the start that he embarked on the history of the war "beginning at the moment that it broke out, and believing that it could be a great war, and more worthy of relation than any that had preceded it." Later on he says: "I have lived through the whole of it, being of an age to comprehend events, and giving my attention to them in order to know the exact truth about them."

Thucydides followed a more disciplined scientific
method than his predecessors, even though they wrote
for the same public. He purged all residues of mythology from his narrative, warning the reader that
"the absence of romance in my history will, I fear,
detract from its interest." Throughout the years he
painstakingly collected precise information about the
war from the most trustworthy sources, eye-witnesses,
documents and treaties, and scrupulously cross-
checked where he could. When, as in the case of a
solar eclipse, he could not explain the causes of an
event, he frankly admitted his ignorance and did not
bring in fancies about the gods to help him out.

He concentrated upon the political relations between
the city-states contending for supremacy in Greece and
adhered strictly to that single theme. The mighty commercial and naval state of Athens was both democratic and imperialistic—and Thucydides rightly
attributed the prolonged Peloponnesian War to the
fear produced among the Lacedemonians by the aggressive expansionist policies of the Athenian mercantile classes.

He carefully distinguished between the official pre-
texts of the combatants for their actions and the underlying political, strategic and economic reasons for their
deep hostility and alliances. He seldom permitted
religious, moral, patriotic or purely personal prejudices
to sway his objective analysis of the causes of events
and the motives of the chief participants.

Thucydides probed realistically into the early history
of Hellenic civilization, the origins of the Mycenean
monarchies, the growth of the Greek city-states and

the rise of the Athenian empire. He correctly connected the rise of the tyrannies with the failure of the established aristocracies and oligarchies to pursue a vigorous policy of overseas colonial and commercial expansion when the leading states were in competition to establish trading posts and areas of exploitation on the margin of the Greek world—and explained the downfall of the tyrannies at the hands of the democratic forces when their narrow autocratic interests blocked the further development of urban prosperity and power.

Thucydides did not penetrate below the level of political realities to their economic bases in a conscious or systematic way and tended to explain the course of events by reference to the personal qualities of individual leaders from Pericles to Alcibiades rather than to the material drives of the conflicting classes and states. Nevertheless, he was the most materialistic of all ancient historians.

For example, he correlated forms of government with the prevailing structure of society and the specific interests of the dominant classes. The "patriarchal monarchy with traditional prerogatives" was the form of rulership corresponding to the pre-political association based on the family and clan. The oligarchy of Corinth was the political counterpart of the social and economic condition of a commercial and maritime state. Sparta's government represented the ascendancy of collectivist landholders over a larger class of "neighbors" who, while politically subordinate, were economically "free" and over a still larger class of ruthlessly exploited and rigidly controlled helots. Finally,

Athenian democracy depended for its existence upon the imperial tribute exacted from subject states which put the old landed aristocracy as well as the large and important middle-class agriculturalists completely at the mercy of the "sea-faring rabble."

Thucydides introduced his description of the terrible plague which devastated besieged Athens in the following manner: "Anyone, physician or layman, may say what he thinks about the probable origins of the plague, and the causes which he thinks were enough to produce so great a disorder. I, for my part, shall describe only what it was like, and record those symptoms which might enable it to be recognized again, if ever it should recur; for I was attacked by it myself, and personally observed others who suffered from it." He then presented a detailed account, not only of the physical manifestations of the epidemic, but also of its mental and moral effects upon the population.

The scientific spirit of his analysis stands in striking contrast to the opening of the *Iliad* where the plague inflicted on the Greek camp is attributed to the anger of the gods and exorcised by appeasing them. The progress of the Greek mind from its nascent expression under barbaric conditions to its maturing in the imperial-democratic commercial city-state can be gauged by comparing these two passages.

These pioneer historians did not develop any thoroughgoing theories of the evolution of society or the laws of its operation. Herodotus assigned the immediate causes of events to the will of individuals and their ultimate causes to Fate or the jealousy of the gods.

Despite his insight into the mainsprings of the struggles he recorded, Thucydides believed that history moved in a cycle which kept repeating itself, just as Plato and Aristotle believed that the planets rotated in recurring harmonious circles. He thought his history would be useful to future generations because what had happened before would come again and be followed by the same consequences. Nevertheless, his cyclical scheme represented the first attempt to uncover a pattern of regularity which could render the historical process as a whole intelligible.

He observed that the Greeks of his time had emerged from tribal institutions and were rooted in the past. "Many proofs might be given to show that the early Greeks had a manner of life similar to that of barbarians today." This discovery that the Greeks stood at a higher level of social development than their ancestors and other peoples and had passed through successive stages of culture was a starting point for comparative history and scientific sociology.

By initiating a method of writing about human affairs which dispensed with supernatural controls and sought to bring all human action within the purview of material causation, Thucydides paved the way for the scientific study of social processes which many centuries later would give birth to historical materialism.

*   *   *

Hippocrates, Democritus and Thucydides were contemporaries. The physician was born in the same year, 460 B.C., though not in the same place, as Democritus and later became his good friend. He was also a pupil of the Sophist Gorgias and another, Protagoras, may have been the author of *Ancient Medicine* in the Hippocratic collection. The principles of the method used by Thucydides were very similar to those of the Hippocratic school.

The Atomistic philosopher, the physician and the historian were all influenced by the materialist traditions of the Ionian naturalists and best reflected in their special fields the materialist trends of the 5th Century B.C. They banished the supernatural in any form and sought for material causes to explain the phenomena which they studied in the physical world, human life and their own civilization.

To them, fortune was no longer the goddess who interfered with the cosmic order and directed the outcome of human affairs; chance was no more than the incalculable element in human life which was governed by necessity and susceptible of rational explanation. Democritus said: "Chance is an idol which men fashioned to excuse their own mental incapacity. As a matter of fact chance seldom conflicts with wisdom. In most affairs of life, an intelligent mind can exercise foresight with success." They shared a basic belief in the existence of natural law and the possibility of scientific knowledge and intelligent action based upon it which is at the core of the materialist outlook.

XI. The Sophists

THE EVOLUTION OF THE materialist outlook has been traced up to this point with only incidental references to the prehistory of the idealist school. It is now necessary to focus attention upon the counter-movement in philosophy to materialism. Since this work is devoted to the topic of materialism, the discussion of idealism and its development will have to be limited largely to its effects upon the course of its antithesis.

Although the materialist tendency crystallized sooner, the idealist standpoint acquired the paramount position in Greece. It was the decisive and triumphant school of thought in the ancient world. Idealism became the ruling ideology because it had the most deep-seated social conditions and powerful class forces sustaining it. Tradition, religion, the requirements of the slave aristocracy, the low level of plebeian

173

culture conspired to direct theory along idealist channels and divert it from materialism.

The idealist school produced some of the most brilliant representatives of human thought who set forth
strong arguments in its favor and systematized its
conceptions into a new and all-embracing world outlook. The idealists gained added advantages from
the shortcomings of materialist theory itself at that
infantile stage of its development.

The broadening stream of Greek speculation from
the 6th to the 4th Centuries took a meandering and
intricate course. The two main contending currents
of philosophy were not sharply counterposed to each
other. They met, merged, commingled, now running
together, now moving apart. The materialist current
was fed by the development of the arts, crafts and
techniques, the diffusion of the money economy, the
class struggles bound up with the democratic revolution and the criticism of religion. Idealism connected
itself with the recasting of religion, the new mathematical discoveries, the mystical cults, and the morals,
legal standards and politics of the slave-owning class.

When we analyze the views of individual philosophers, the two strains of thought are to be found
mixed in varying proportions in almost all of them.
Thales, the father of materialism, still conceived of
the principle of life, movement and dynamism in
terms of the gods. On the other hand, Plato, the peer-
less idealist, showed himself to be a keen student of
the actual constitutions and political life of the chief
Greek city-states, Sparta, Athens and Syracuse, even
in the projection of his dream-city in *The Republic*.

He tried to sketch a lawful progression in the development of successive forms of the state from oligarchy through democracy to tyranny and ascribes these political transformations in part to changes in the distribution of wealth and property.

Moreover, there are marked differences amongst the advocates of idealism themselves. Socrates, the son of a sculptor and midwife, was closer to the technical spirit of the craftsmen than Plato, his disciple; while Aristotle, the systematizer of idealism, displayed a gradual drift away from the unalloyed idealism of Plato toward materialism as his thinking progressed.

This does not mean that it is impossible or unnecessary to distinguish the one tendency from the other. The Greeks themselves were well aware that the two standpoints were opposed to each other. The essential position of the various schools and philosophers was determined by which trend was dominant and which recessive in the body of their ideas.

The Pythagoreans and Eleatics, for example, definitely belonged among the precursors of idealism because their principal doctrines—that the universe is essentially constituted of number and that the logical is the real—were anti-materialist. It is true that the world has mathematical properties; it is also true that reality is logical and logic is real. But the conclusions of the Pythagoreans and the Eleatics that the essence of reality is mathematical and logical rather than material is the antithesis of materialism.

Conversely, the Milesian naturalists and the Atomists have to be placed in the materialist camp, despite the vestiges of religious notions and other inconsistencies in their ideas, because their fundamental methods of explanation and doctrines were primarily based upon such physical realities as states of matter, one of the four elements, or on atoms and empty space.

◩ Anaxagoras

OTHER THINKERS CAN BE classified accordingly. Anaxagoras provides a good test. He taught that *Nous* (spirit or mind) which moves and knows all things, was the cause of motion. Were we to single out this one aspect of his thought, he would appear to be ranged on the side of idealism. The earliest materialists took for granted that motion was inherent in nature and therefore had no reason to bring forward any originator for the movement of things.

But to inflate that one feature of Anaxagoras' thought out of proportion would lead to a superficial and incorrect appraisal of the major orientation of his views. As Aristotle pointed out, Anaxagoras only used the notion of "Mind as a *deus ex machina* to account for the formation of the world; and whenever he is at a loss to explain why anything necessarily is, he drags it in. But in other cases he makes anything rather than Mind the cause." The meaning of this criticism is plain. When Anaxagoras was able to offer a positive explanation of any phenomenon, he reasoned along materialist lines and kept mind as the prime mover on the shelf. But when he did not know the specific causes of things and was at a loss to account for them otherwise, he dragged in *Nous* as a means of explanation. That is to say, *Nous* served as an expression of his ignorance.

177

The contrast between Anaxagoras and Aristotle comes out in their views on the development of mankind's own intelligence. Anaxagoras said that man acquired intelligence because he had hands. This is a substantially correct and materialistically founded explanation. Aristotle combats this theory and says that hands were given to men because he had intelligence. This is a teleological explanation in the idealist manner because it has human intelligence originate in the volition of a superhuman intelligence.

Further testimony on this score is given by Plato. He has Socrates say in *The Phaedo:* "I once heard someone reading from a book (as he said) by Anaxagoras, and asserting that it is mind that produces order and is the cause of everything. This explanation pleased me. Somehow it seemed right that mind should be the cause of everything . . . It was a wonderful hope, my friend, but it was quickly dashed. As I read on I discovered that the fellow made no use of Mind and assigned to it no causality for the order of the world, but adduced causes like air and ether and water and many other absurdities."

Socrates' disappointment with Anaxagoras and aversion to his trend of thought is particularly pertinent to our purpose. First, Anaxagoras (*ca.* 500-428 B.C.) was a living link between the Milesian naturalists and the classical Athenian idealists. He was the first foreign philosopher to take up residence in Athens where he stayed for thirty years. He came there after his native city Klazomenai had been destroyed following the crushing of the revolt of the Ionian Greeks against the Persian despotism. He was closely associated with Pericles, the illustrious leader of Athenian democracy, but was tried and expelled from Athens on charges of treasonable collaboration with the Persians because of his association with the Periclean party and on charges of impiety because he taught that the sun was a red-hot stone and the moon was made of earth.

Second, the idealists, beginning with Socrates, took seriously, applied consistently and elevated to first place in their scheme of explanation the very principle of *Nous*, the intelligence, which Anaxagoras had kept subordinate.

⊡ The Sophists

ANOTHER PHILOSOPHER WHO served as a link between the materialists and idealists was Protagoras, the chief of the Sophists. He was a pupil of Democritus, a contemporary of Anaxagoras, a teacher of Socrates, and a friend of Pericles.

The Sophists came forward at the height of the democratic movement which had originated in the Ionian trading centers a hundred and fifty years earlier. During the second half of the 5th Century the people became fully sovereign under Pericles in Athens.

This democratic revolution which transferred power from the landed aristocracy to the commercial and manufacturing classes had given birth to philosophy in its youth; the doctrines of the Atomists and of the Sophists were characteristic philosophical products of its maturity.

The ascending democracy, surging ahead with the impetuous growth of wealth, trade and industry, reconstructed the state and swept aside its most time-honored institutions. In Athens, for example, the council of the Areopagus, the highest court of judgment for the gravest offenses, was replaced by paid juries. The overthrow of this mainstay of aristocratic rule by democratic law courts open to the poorest citizens showed the Athenians that not even the most sacrosanct features of their society were untouchable or unchangeable.

The Areopagus was both a civil and a religious organ under the special protection of the deities. The Hill of Ares on which it sat was holy; the Furies were thought to dwell at its foot; and its sessions were held in the open air so that no one might be polluted by coming into the same chamber with a person guilty of shedding blood. Its demotion delivered a double blow at the privileges of the nobility and the hold of traditional religion.

Periclean Athens created remarkable works of art and produced some of the most gifted personalities of antiquity. But it was the home of newly enriched entrepreneurs who had little respect for the ancient ways and were driven by an exorbitant greed for gain and imperialist ambitions. Their assaults upon the moral, legal and political supports of the old order came to a head in the Peloponnesian War through which the struggle between the democrats and oligarchs were extended throughout Greece.

"The whole Hellenic world was convulsed, struggles being everywhere made by the popular chiefs to bring in the Athenians, and by the oligarchs to introduce the Lacedaemonians," wrote Thucydides who participated in these revolutionary events and described them from the standpoint of "the moderate part of its citizens." "The leaders in the cities, each provided with the fairest professions, on the one side with the cry of political equality of the people, on the other side of a moderate aristocracy, sought props for themselves in those public interests which they pretended to cherish, engaged in the direst excesses . . . Morality was in honor

with neither party . . . Every form of ini-
quity took root."

The Sophists tried to meet the demand for a new
intellectual orientation among the educated classes in
this turbulent age of city-state wars, democratic revolutions and oligarchic counterrevolutions when everything was unsettled and placed in doubt. These learned
men have fallen into disrepute in later history until
today their name is a byword for twisted reasoning
and counterfeit philosophy. This is an injustice initiated by the conservatives of their time and perpetuated
by the echoers of the classical idealists. The Sophists
were slandered in their day just as the Encyclopedists
of the 18th Century were execrated by the upholders of the old regime and misrepresented by
19th Century reactionaries. Aristophanes, the comic
playwright, did much to give the Sophists a
bad name by his lampoon of Socrates in *The
Clouds*.

The Sophists were itinerant foreign thinkers who
travelled from place to place, seeking audiences, clients, and spreading new ideas. They were attracted
to Athens by its wealth, eminence and vigorous intellectual and scientific activity. Like other tradesmen,
some of them now and then palmed off inferior
goods with flashy labels upon a gullible public. But
the leading Sophists were not shallow and mercenary
thinkers who improvised specious arguments for im-
proper purposes; they were influential innovators in
the Greek culture of the 5th Century.

By broadening the concepts and curriculum of
learning, these pioneers in Western education opened

the doors of knowledge, hitherto monopolized by the aristocracy, to larger layers of the people. They proclaimed that learning was not the natural endowment of good breeding but could be acquired by everyone who exercised his intelligence. They encouraged an attitude which subjected dogmas, myths, superstitions to critical examination.

In their own way these specialists in history and politics, who professed to prepare the sons of the well-born and the well-to-do for adult life and success in public affairs, were abettors of social reform. Protagoras was a legislator, who, at the request of Pericles, helped establish a model colony in South Italy, the first planned town.

The Sophists were scorned by spokesmen for the patricians because they took fees for their services. But this feature of their professional activities which offended aristocratic etiquette suited the customs of a money economy. The urban commercial democracies called upon these educators for a new type of education.

The old educational ideal which found its perfect expression in Sparta was based on the training of a military elite. It exalted aristocratic ways of life, chivalric contests, the cultivation of manly sports, bodily exercise.

The Sophists introduced a mode of education more adapted to the needs and virtues of the democratic republics. Their emphasis upon developing knowledge, training the mind in logical thinking, improving speech, participating in political discussion was designed to produce not simply disciplined warriors

but critical-minded individuals able to speak force-
fully and to the point in order to convince their
fellow citizens of the correct course of action.

Such skills were required not only by leaders of
the democratic forces but even more by their opponents who had to contend with them in the assemblies and the law courts. Once the political hegemony
of the aristocracy was shattered, their representatives
who aspired to direct the city as statesmen, generals,
and magistrates, could win popular favor for their
policies and hold it only by mastering the arts of
public debate.

This new type of philosopher found a public ready
to pay for his abilities because life in the democratic
city-states fostered discussion in the market-places,
debate in the Assemblies, confrontation of opposing
sides in the law courts. The clash of antagonistic
property interests, the incessant bargaining in the
marts of trade, the fierce contentions of political factions, the informal meetings of citizens in the public
places stimulated the interplay of ideas among the
governing elements of all tendencies. The methods of
the Sophists and Socrates or a literary form like
Plato's *Dialogues.* which turned upon the thrust and
parry of opposing arguments, would be inconceiv-
able in an Oriental despotism which had neither a
thriving mercantile activity nor a politically independent and energetic body of free citizens. They came
out of an environment where goods, money and ideas
were extensively exchanged and class conflicts were
open and heated.

The Sophists specialized in studying the techniques

of thought and the modes of speech and made valuable contributions to philosophy through their discoveries in rhetoric and grammar. They helped prepare several elements for the science of logic which was created by the outstanding figures of Greek idealism.

The "antilogical" method of the Sophists clearly reproduced in theory the upheavals and conflicts of their time. They asserted that in every experience two "logoi" were in opposition to each other; every thesis had its antithesis. The Sophists taught their students how to bring out the opposition to any given position and make, if necessary, the weaker appear the stronger side.

They demonstrated that differing views, customs, and institutions in religion, politics, ethics, and economics were equally justifiable. Here are some of the contradictory opinions given in the *Disoi Logoi,* written after the Peloponnesian War, which illustrate how the same actions and events could be appraised in diametrically different ways according to the circumstances of the situation and the standpoint and interests of the evaluator.

"Immoderate consumption of food and drink is bad for the immoderate consumer, but good for the tradesman. Victory at the games is good for the victor, but bad for the defeated. The issue of the Peloponnesian War was good for the Lacedaemonians, but bad for the Athenians.

"To put on finery and cosmetics is indecent for a man, but decent for a woman. In Macedonia it is decent for a girl to have premarital relations, in Hellas it is not.

"To deceive an enemy is just, to deceive a friend is unjust. Murder of relations is unjust, but sometimes, as in the case of Orestes, it is just. Temple robbery is unjust, but to take the treasure of Delphi when Hellas is threatened by the barbarians is just."

Such an approach to phenomena tended to unsettle all things and to deprive entrenched customs, standards and institutions of their universality and necessity. Nothing appeared forever fixed; no truths were absolutely certain; all values were relative.

How, then, could one tell right from wrong, good from bad, true from false, wise from foolish, just from unjust? And how could such knowledge be attained or could it be attained at all?

Protagoras answered that the one side could not be separated from its other. The just was also unjust, the courageous cowardly, the true false depending upon the specific conditions of the individual.

Protagoras was one of the foremost exponents of relativism and subjectivism in ancient Greece. Relativism is that type of thought which fixes upon the changeability of things and the diversity of their appearances to the exclusion or detriment of their essential lawfulness and real necessity.

His point of view pivoted upon two principal propositions.

1. Man is the measure of all things: of the being of those that are and the not-being of those that are not.

2. Contradictory assertions are equally true.

On such a basis things were to each person just as they appeared to him; all sensations, all notions were relative, individual and arbitrary. There can be no common knowledge of an independent material reality, no objective truth. It is impossible to know what things really are in themselves since they appear so very different to different animals, different men, different senses, and under such varying circumstances as age, health, situation, etc. Therefore contradictory assertions about anything can be equally true—or untrue.

Another important Sophist, Gorgias, sharpened this same point by defending the following theses: there is no truth; if there were, it could not be known; if known, it could not be communicated.

The relativistic doctrine of Protagoras that man is the measure of all things did not have a purely theoretical character; it also served practical social purposes. This line of argumentation reinforced the idea that social institutions are not unalterable but can and should be remodeled with the changing requirements of mankind.

Protagoras denied that there were any timeless, abstract and absolute norms of justice, truth, morality and law apart from the needs and outlooks of this or that social group. Law was made for man, not man for the law. Such a theoretical viewpoint acted as a dissolvent upon political structures and religious orthodoxy. Protagoras wrote a book on the gods in which the very first sentence declared that he did not know whether the gods did or did not exist or what they were like.

If right and wrong, justice and injustice, truth and falsehood have no objective and necessary sanction,

then the state and its laws can be founded upon nothing except force or convention. Thrasymachus drew
the conclusion that the laws of the state were inventions of the weak to control the strong and that force
is the only law which nature recognizes.

His assertion that "might is right" horrified those
who sought to veil the role of force in upholding
class society with religious and ethical absolutes. But
Thrasymachus simply exposed what was happening
before the eyes of all Greece where one government
after another was being knocked down and set up
by force and fraud and the strength of the contending
forces was the only law. The idealists could not forgive the more outspoken Sophists for tearing aside
the fig-leaves from the realities of power in their
commercial slave regimes.

In his *Sisyphus*, Critias treated religion in an equally
iconoclastic manner. Once society had been brought
under the reign of law, he said, someone "persuaded
the mortals to believe in the existence of a race of
gods" to surround them with fear and keep them
law-abiding.

Other Sophists undermined conservatism by counterposing nature to custom or law. Antiphon contended
that most of what is considered just according to rules
of law is contrary to nature. Aristotle attributed extremely levelling sentiments to certain Sophistic authors: "It is against nature to be another man's master,
for only by law is one man a slave, another a freeman; by nature they do not differ; the rule of the
master over slave is based on force, and, therefore,
not just."

The Sophists displayed a strong materialist bent by stressing the role of historical social conditions in making men what they were. In common with the Atomists, the Hippocratics, the historians and the dramatists, they looked upon mankind as essentially a creative craftsman whose inventive skills were responsible for the achievements of civilization.

The sole significant new idea on the nature of the physical world contributed by the Sophists came from Antisthenes, the pupil of Gorgias and Prodicus. He was the first Greek thinker to identify being explicitly with material body. He stated that only individuals exist and only corporeal things sensitive to the touch were real. The qualities of objects perceived by the senses, detached from the substantial being that contained them, were unreal.

His theory of knowledge was the antithesis to that of the idealists who abstracted qualities from things and transformed them into independently existing entities. Antisthenes is reported to have remarked: "O Plato, I see a horse, but I do not see horseness."

This view of matter as extended and resistant substance was not widespread in antiquity, although it later passed into the Stoic view of nature. However, the conception of matter faintly foreshadowed by Antisthenes was to become a keystone in the mechanical system of nature which dominated the bourgeois epoch.

Although the Sophists consorted with the upper classes and did not champion the most radical opinions, the restless criticism of their dialectical method made the conservatives detest and mistrust them. Their teachings were supposed to corrupt the youth and subvert morality, political stability, and religion.

The classical idealists took the techniques of logic devised by the Sophists and turned them into weapons for a systematic counter-offensive against their relativism, individualism, skepticism and subjectivism. Socrates argued against the Sophists that the just and the lawful were the same. Plato maintained against Protagoras that not man but God was the measure of all things. He wished to reserve rulership to the best whereas the Sophists were willing to impart statecraft to any rational person. They undertook to offset the liberalizing influence of the Sophists by finding absolute and invariable standards in philosophy, logic, ethics and politics which could restabilize the positions and values of the oligarchy imperiled by the triumphant democratic movement.

XII. Athens
and the Socratic Revolution

SOCRATES LIVED FROM 469 TO 399; Plato from 427 to 347; Aristotle from 384 to 322 B.C. All three centered their philosophical activities in Athens. They were affiliated with one another and formed a continuity of idealist thought stretching over a hundred years.

The development of idealism cannot be understood apart from the evolution of Athens during the 5th and 4th Centuries because these classical idealists were among the supreme representatives of its culture.

🔲 The Life of Athens

THE GREEK CITIES had emerged from tribal and village conditions in which most other peoples and even some retarded Greek communities still lived. They were soon to pass under the subordination of the Alexandrian empire. But in the 5th Century they attained the height of their power, independence and achievements.

The commercial interests and ambitions of the Athenians had enabled and impelled them to take the foremost part in the wars against Persia which saved Greece from the danger of Oriental domination. The Athenians aided the Asiatic Greeks in their revolt against the Persian king Darius; Athenian forces conquered the Persian invaders at Marathon and her fleet assured the victory over the admirals of Xerxes at Salamis. Athens, the savior of Greece, became the center of the pan-Hellenic Confederacy; the Aegan became an Athenian lake as its rule was extended over Megara and Boeotia.

But, at the peak of its power, Athens became involved in a prolonged war with its rival Sparta which lasted with interruptions from 431 to 404 B.C. and ended in the defeat and downfall of the Athenian Empire. The humbled Athenians never regained their hegemony over Greece.

The internal history of Athens was as dramatic and turbulent as its foreign relations. During both its upward and downward course its career was marked by fast-moving overturns. Thanks to its prosperity and power, the city became architecturally transformed; art, literature, philosophy, history flourished. With the push given by its plebeian and maritime population, the Athenian constitution became the most democratic in Greece. In the Athens of Socrates' time stages of progress which required centuries elsewhere were compressed within a few generations. The bewildering rapidity of these changes, the extremely compressed character of the historical development and the startling reversals at home and abroad inspired the most strenuous exertions and liveliest thoughts among its leading inhabitants.

Athens, even more than the other advanced cities of Greece, incorporated sharp contrasts. It was part urban and part rural, although the city dominated the country; part old and part new; part free and part slave. Production for use was intermixed with production for exchange. Agriculture and stockraising were carried on side by side with mining and rapidly developing industry, trade and banking. Early tribal customs, ideas and institutions blended with social, political and economic innovations. Freedom and self-government for its citizens clashed in theory and in practice with enslavement and disfranchisement at home and imperialist expansion abroad.

These paradoxical combinations and the violent contradictions arising from them imparted a tremendous dynamism to the development of Athens and keenly edged the minds of its inhabitants. A. D. Godley writes: "The city . . . was always eager to hear or tell of some new thing. It was a period of intellectual awakening, when, as in the Elizabethan and in our own era, new ideas and new discoveries (discoveries then, at least, of untrodden continents of the intellect) were daily widening the field of discussion. The vehicle of criticism was not writing, but conversation. Wit encountered wit in actual speech.

"And several causes operated to make Athens beyond all Greek towns a conversational center. Her political importance, as well as her theatrical exhibitions, brought crowds of strangers from all parts of Greece, the Aegean, nay, from the Western outposts of Hellenic civilizations—from Sicily itself and the Greek towns of Southern Italy. Even the hardships of the Peloponnesian War had their effect in this direction, as the fear of the Peloponnesian raiders more and more centralized Attic life within the walls of the metropolis of Athens. So in Athens, the most diverse elements might find a meeting place: country gentlemen driven from their estates by the terror of invading armies; islanders bringing tribute from the Aegean; travelling professors from Southern Italy or Asia Minor—all alike contributing after their several fashions new points of view and new elements of discussion."—*Socrates and Athenian Society* (pp. 36-37).

Athens had a population of from three to four hundred thousand at the peak of its prosperity. It was the principal manufacturing, mercantile and financial center of Greece. Its inhabitants engaged in the most diverse occupations. Outside the city walls peasants grew corn, olives and grapes for wine; shepherds tended flocks in the hills. Within the city, craftsmen, free and slave, made many kinds of articles for sale from leather goods to pottery. Four miles away was the port of Piraeus, the scene of a bustling export and import trade and shipbuilding, connected by walls with the city. Not far, in the hills of Laurion, were the silver mines where twenty thousand slaves extracted the precious metals which provided a large measure of Athens' revenue.

The monetary economy of Athens had travelled very far from the old self-contained village community. This cosmopolis was dependent upon foreign imports for its food and upon exports for its prosperity. Its far-flung economic base made it the diplomatic, military and naval power of the first rank in the Mediterranean and plunged it into wars against such enemies of Greece as Persia and such rival city-states as Sparta and Corinth.

The highly developed economy of Athens accounted for the variegated hierarchy of its social structure. In the countryside, rich landlords and noble families were arrayed against small farmers, pastoralists and miners; within the city, manufacturers, merchants, shipowners, financiers and professional people jostled artisans, mechanics, maritime workers and sailors. Unlike 6th Century Miletus, trade in 4th Century Athens was largely concentrated in the hands of non-citizens and based on moneylenders' capital.

The inhabitants were divided into nobles and commoners, native-born citizens and alien non-citizens, rich and poor, freemen and slaves. The citizens with their wives and children roughly numbered about 160,000; resident aliens about 90,000; slaves 80,000.

Rich and high-born Athenians possessed large numbers of slaves and owed their wealth and leisure to
them. Even artisans and small proprietors owned
and employed slaves. The state itself was the largest
employer of slaves, exploiting them in the mines and
galleys and using them as policemen and clerks.

The chattels were sometimes of Greek origin but
usually of foreign birth. Their conditions varied
considerably from terrible treatment in the mines and
work-gangs to more lenient use as domestic servants
and skilled craftsmen who brought profit to their
owners. Slaves served as teachers; the principal
banker of Athens was once a slave.

The Athenian economy rose on the pedestal of slavery at home and imperial subjugation abroad. This
form of property and mode of production penetrated
every aspect and avenue of Athenian life and placed
an indelible stamp upon the ideas of its intellectuals.

Politically Athens was a slave democracy. Since
Cleisthenes, the city had been divided into two hundred demes, or wards, which combined features of the
ancient tribal kinship system with the new civilized
type of organization based upon territorial residence.
The old tribal divisions retained a ceremonial character. The city had a common cult; the town hall
was likewise the town hearth. Birth remained the pass-
port to citizenship. Only those whose father and mother
were legitimately married Athenian citizens had a
share in political life.

As early as 570 B.C. Athens had been divided into
three parties: the Coast party of the large and small
merchants, who aimed at a middle-class republic;

the Plains party, based on the big landed estates of the best farming districts, who wanted an oligarchy; and the Hill party, the most radical and democratic, which mobilized the poorer peasants, miners, shepherds and artisans behind progressive industrialists and merchants and became the driving force behind the democratic cause. From that time on, there was ceaseless struggle between the forces of aristocratic reaction and the democratic camp which culminated in eventual victory for the people and the establishment of the democratic republic.

This republic was governed by a council of 500, elected by lot by ten tribal groups, each embracing one-tenth of the demes. It did not have any supreme executive like an ancient king or modern mayor, governor nor president. All citizens were obliged to participate in public affairs. Athens governed and defended herself through the rotating services of 7,000 out of 40,000 citizens. One of every six citizens was regularly engaged in daily duties for the state, either civil or military. Under Pericles they were paid for their services in the army or navy, for attending the Council or hearing cases in the law courts. This enabled the commoners, craftsmen and maritime workers to administer public affairs directly and keep informed about all problems of the state from diplomatic negotiations to legal litigation.

Even though the wealth, leisure and democracy of Athens rested upon slavery, and women and foreigners were excluded from political life, it must be recognized that within these historical limitations equality, freedom and self government were unsurpassed among its citizens.

The keynote of Athenian reality was not calm but strife. The prolonged and victorious wars of national defense had heightened the pride, self-confidence and respect of the Athenians; the intrigues and imperialist wars with rival city-states stimulated where it did not lay waste their energies; the vast ramifications of their commercial and colonizing enterprises, the disputes of litigants before the law tribunals, election contests, factional struggles and civil overturns contributed to the commotion of life. The envoy for the Corinthians told the Lacedaemonians that the Athenians "were born into the world to take no rest themselves and to give none to others."

This applied with full force to the gadfly Socrates who developed his ideas and methods in this social setting. Socrates never wrote or published anything; our knowledge of his teachings is derived from contemporaries like Aristophanes, disciples like Plato and Xenophon and critics like Aristotle. (Some scholars, like Storey, see more of Plato than Socrates in the *Dialogues*; others, such as John Burnet and A.E. Taylor, attribute to Socrates himself all ideas expressed by the Platonic Socrates up to and including the *Republic* with its theory of Ideal Forms.)

He resembled the Sophists in his mode of activity, as a teacher of the upper-class youth, a critic of prevailing conventions, and the center of a circle of friends which included some of the foremost citizens of Athens. The Socratic method is an extension and refinement of the innovations of the Sophists. They were jointly responsible for shifting the axis of philosophy from inquiry into nature to a concentration upon human nature and conduct, from the objective to the subjective side of reality.

But Socrates was extremely critical of the other leading Sophists and worked out his own positions in polemics with them. He became the pivotal personality in the evolution of Greek philosophy because he was the acknowledged founder of idealism. With him the swing away from materialism was conclusively effected. Socrates was the engineer who guided the train of philosophy onto the tracks of idealism, the main line on which it has subsequently travelled.

This epoch-making switch is justly called "the Socratic Revolution." In recognition of this strategic turning point, Greek philosophy is customarily divided into the pre-Socratic, the classical, and the post-Aristotlian periods. This classification, made from the idealist standpoint, does an injustice to the Atomists by shunting them off on a side-track. But it does reflect the fact that henceforth idealism was predominant, and materialism subordinate, in Greek thought.

The Socratic revolution in philosophy issued from the convulsive struggles between the democracy and the oligarchy. Socrates spent all seventy years of his life in Athens and rarely went beyond its walls. He fought three times in the army and served as a public commissioner.

He went through the Peloponnesian War, saw his city reach the heights, then fight with its back to the wall until it was uncrowned as queen of the Mediterranean world. After the death of Pericles, he saw his intimate friend and disciple, Alcibiades, assume direction of the policies of the state. He saw the anti-democratic leaders take advantage of the defeats and distress suffered by the Athenians to institute an oligarchic dictatorship in 413 and again under the " Thirty" when the war was lost in 404.

Socrates was not a spokesman for the people nor an advocate of democratic ideas. Suspected of aristocratic sympathies, he was condemned to death in 399 B.C. by partisans of the democratic camp. But he fashioned his notions in the atmosphere of the popular movement. His rationalism, individualism, humanism and critical spirit accorded with tendencies generated by the democratic forces. On the other hand his idealist theories and aristocratic bias expressed the upper-class reaction against the levelling tendencies of the urban "rabble."

⌘ The Socratic Revolution

WHAT WAS THE NATURE OF the revolution Socrates initiated in Greek philosophy?

For purposes of analysis, reality can be divided into three distinct though materially interconnected spheres: the external world, or nature; human society; and the mind. At different phases of its development philosophy has centered attention upon one or another of these sectors. The Milesians were almost wholly concerned with the processes of nature, or rather, they did not make any sharp distinctions between the various divisions of reality or analyze to any extent either society or the thought process.

"Down to the middle of the 5th Century," says Professor Robin, "the object of philosophical thought had been to say what is the underlying reality, and what is the true being, of the visible universe. Reflection on conduct had been left to poets and lawgivers and philosophy had not regarded it as one of its proper objects."—*Greek Thought and the Origins of the Scientific Spirit* (p. 131).

With the Sophists and Socrates a more advanced level of theory was reached. They differentiated society as an object distinct from nature and began to examine social relations and human conduct in a scientific way.

This shift from the investigation of nature to the study of mankind may appear at first glance to be

a retreat from science. It is true that Socrates relegated inquiry into nature to the background and
even regarded it as worthless in philosophical questions but there were more positive aspects to this turn
in philosophy than a mere aversion to further investigation of the external world. Although he came to
idealistic conclusions, Socrates investigated the nature of society and the conduct of mankind in a
naturalistic way without appealing to religious sanc-
tions or relying on established custom. "Human life
was analyzed as physiologists dissect a frog, and the
result was a secular, unmetaphysical ethics."

This was a step forward for philosophy. Socrates
extended the circumference of rational thought to
cover social life, giving philosophy an explicitly political aim and combining critical thought with social
practice.

The fact that the center of theoretical interest was
displaced from the natural to the social environment
was not in itself a sign of retrogression, as it is
sometimes interpreted. It was rather an expression
of the deep need felt by the contending forces in the
leading city-states to find answers to a series of unpost-
ponable moral, political and theoretical problems. *

---

* We can note a comparable emphasis upon the solution of social problems in
such philosophies as Marxism which aimed first of all to provide answers for the
movement of the modern working class, or the pragmatism of John Dewey which
was the philosophical instrument of the Progressive movement in the United States.
Incidentally, that is why Dewey felt so strong a sympathy with the accent upon morality and social problems to be found in Socrates.

The great reversal which Socrates instituted in philosophy on behalf of the Athenian aristocracy beset by the democratic movement was to subordinate nature to mankind in theory by reinterpreting natural processes on the model of human activity and human reasoning. What the primitives had done in a spontaneous way through magic and primitive animism Socrates reproduced in an entirely different and wholly rational form on the higher level of civilization.

The Ionian "physiologists" proceeded from natural laws to human life; Socrates proceeded from human thought and social activity to nature. As Lange has remarked: "His entire conviction is that the reason which has created the world structure proceeds after the manner of human reason; that we can follow its thoughts everywhere, although we must at the same time admit its infinite superiority. The world is explained from man, not man from the universal laws of nature. In the order of natural events, then, there is presupposed throughout that antithesis of thoughts and acts, of plan and material execution, which we find in our own consciousness."—(p. 64).

For Socrates, mankind was created by a supreme and intelligent craftsman who contrived the rest of the world to serve our needs. He pointed out how God, or the highest Good, has taken care to provide mankind with light, water, fire and air. The sun shines by day and the moon and the stars by night to give light to mankind. The earth produces food and other necessities for our sustenance and the animals exist to serve mankind. The human organism and its organs equally prove the wide foresight of the benevolent creator. "Are not these eyelids provided as it were with a fence on the edge of them to keep off the wind and guard the eye? Even the eyebrow itself is not without its office, but, as a penthouse is prepared to turn off the sweat, which, falling from the forehead, might enter and annoy that no less tender than astonishing part of us."

This is a thoroughly teleological conception of reality which sees the evidences of intelligent purpose and divine handiwork everywhere. It is unabashed, unalloyed idealism. The universe is animated by purpose and guided by reason. This specific rational purpose is modelled upon the social position and outlook of Athenian aristocrats. God takes care of the needs of mankind and especially its philosophical elite, just as the material needs of these men of leisure were taken care of by others.

If Socrates established this idealistic view of the cosmos, he is no less the founder of a rational doctrine of morality and the creator of a systematic theory of knowledge. Declaring that "the unexamined life is not worth living" he sought to subject human conduct and social institutions to rigorous criticism by reason.

The ethical theory of Socrates is bound up with his theory of knowledge. Knowledge is not only the means to right conduct in life; it is the very essence of morality. Virtue is knowledge. No one does wrong willingly or consciously. Men fall into evil ways because they do not know what the right or the good is.

Virtue comes from true knowledge and all true knowledge must proceed from correct conceptions.

Thus Socrates hinges his whole philosophy upon true knowledge which can be acquired only through the criticism of prevailing ideas. Morals depend upon logic.

This is a long way from the customary morality of ancient Greece or the morality based upon the divine origin of the Ten Commandments of the Israelites as interpreted by priests and prophets. Although aristocratic in substance, Socrates aimed to put morality upon rational foundations.

Socrates had a distinctive method of thought. It started from the assumption that there are two different kinds of knowledge: the ordinary, unexamined opinions of people and the methodical, conscious, true conceptions of the philosophical mind that has uncovered the Good in each case. This Socratic "elenchus" is a means of separating false from true knowledge and arriving at real knowledge by a critical examination of the basis of our beliefs.

The "physiologists" of Ionia had tried to find out the truth by investigating nature and the nature of things themselves. Socrates took a different tack. Instead of a direct investigation of the *facts,* he examined the *statements* which people made or the *theories* which they held about them. He started with some proposition which is presumably or provisionally true. He treats this as an initial hypothesis which will lead through the course of contradiction to a final or self-evident truth.

Taking this initial proposition, he proceeds to deduce its logical consequences. In the course of further discussion, other aspects of the situation are brought forward until opposing views confront one another. The aim of this dialectical method of eliciting counterposing views on the same question is to draw out the consequences of each side in order to see which is true. The result of this debate, dialogue or many-sided dialectical development of ideas is genuine knowledge as contrasted with mere opinion.

Unlike certain Sophists and skeptics, Socrates had no doubt that it is possible and necessary to achieve certain knowledge and the truth about things. In the *Phaedo* he expressly warns against misology, that is, a distrust in the outcome of valid reasoning. He undertakes a dialectical examination of any topic in order to arrive at secure and validated knowledge of its real nature.

In reaction against the Sophists, who stressed the relativity of morals, values, laws, etc., Socrates used his method to distinguish the necessary, the permanent, and the universal from what was contingent, transitory and individual in ideas. He aimed to discover the intelligible in the sensible, the essential in the accidental manifestations.

He tried to attain this by the rational process of generalization which ends in a definition of the given thing. This definition is the true form or the real cause of its being. Anything beautiful, for example, is a manifestation of the form of Beauty itself.

In the last analysis, the idea of the Good, and all other absolute ideas or eternal forms of being were, for Socrates, inborn in the soul, which carried the memory of them from a previous state of existence into this world. All knowledge is recollection, recovery or recognition of the eternal forms.

Socrates' theory of knowledge becomes the gateway to a completely idealistic theory of a reality higher than the material world which mankind experiences through the senses. In the *Phaedo* he set forth two conceptions which henceforth formed the stock in trade of philosophical idealism. These are the doctrines of the divinity and immortality of the soul and the theory of the autonomously existing forms of ideal being. These two key ideas support each other. Belief in the soul's immortality is propped up by the theory of ideal forms which are equally eternal; the theory of ideal forms depends upon the activity of the soul apart from the body.

Socrates created the conception of the soul which is the essence of idealism and which in one guise or another: spirit, mind, absolute idea, has dominated European theology and idealist philosophy since. The doctrine of the soul popularized and perpetuated by Christianity was borrowed from Graeco-Roman culture, which owed it to Socrates.

The roots of this belief in an immaterial other self go far back into savagery. In Homer the psyche or soul is a ghost present in a man as long as he lives and which leaves him at death. Among the Ionians and with Heraclitus, the soul is identified with the air or fire. The early Pythagoreans transformed the psyche into a permanent individuality which has fallen from its former divine state and must practice rules of life which will restore it to its place among the gods.

Socrates took these old ideas and reshaped them.

He identified the soul as the source and seat of both knowledge and goodness. He was the first to rational- ize the concept of the soul and make it that element in human beings which has knowledge and ignorance and can distinguish between virtue and vice. He secu- larized the soul by identifying it with the normal consciousness and character of people, and at the same time, he spiritualized knowledge and conduct by identifying these modes of human activity with a divine entity.

The business of this divine constituent in mankind, the soul, is to know; that is, to apprehend the essence of things in the Forms, and above all, to know good and evil. It will thereby govern a man's action so that he will lead a good life on earth and win eternal bliss.

This doctrine implies a radical division in the kinds of reality and in each individual between the soul and the body. The soul is mind alone, divine, imperish- able, and can exist independently of the body. The body is dragged down by matter, befuddled by appe- tites and emotions which block access to real know- ledge. The visible body has affinity with the visible world of changing physical phenomena, while the soul has intercourse with the invisible pre-existing realm of unchanging and divine forms. The composite body is subject to generation, decay and death; the indivis- ible soul is ungenerated, indestructible and immortal.

The contrast between the eternal Forms and their perishable appearances forms the counterpart in the field of being to this division between the soul and body. Justice is not a merely relative, individual or conventional judgment, varying with time, place and circumstance, as the Sophists contended. Like all other Forms such as Goodness, Evil, Evenness and Straightness, Justice is absolute, universal, eternally pre-existing, objective. It never changes but is an absolutely invariable standard.

Socrates and Plato candidly acknowledged that their arguments on behalf of the immortality of the soul and the eternity of the Forms were designed to buttress "the old and sacred stories which reveal to us that souls are immortal." The innovation of the idealists consisted in the method by which they rescued and rehabilitated these antique beliefs. They did not resort to tradition, although they paid respects to that, or to institutional authority or dogmatic deliverance to establish their conclusions. They tried to base them upon argumentation and an appeal to the most highly critical reason.

This can be clearly seen in the *Phaedo* where Socrates through Plato seeks to prove immortality by a series of theoretical arguments. These range from demonstrating the cyclical process of birth and death and the inevitable alteration of opposite states of being to the final demonstration that the theory of Forms proves the soul indestructible, since Forms do not have any internal opposition or self-contradiction. All these arguments are brought forward against the objections of friendly critics or opponents. Reason and logical demonstration are given the last word.

*   *   *

The contributions of Socrates to philosophy can be summed up as follows:

On the one hand, he laid the basis for the science of logic. Aristotle credits him with introducing inductive arguments and universal definitions. He gave the first examples of a scientific treatment of moral problems and of an intimate unity of critical theory with social practice. For Socrates, enlightenment, will and conduct are all integrated; the test of true knowledge is a proved capacity for correct action.

On the other hand, Socrates turned away from objective inquiry into nature and interpreted the world teleologically. He reinforced religion with his conception of the immortal soul, temporarily inhabiting a house of clay. He explained human history as a display of divine providence rather than as the self-development of mankind in the struggle for survival under given conditions. He developed the theory of eternal ideas and absolute Forms which stood above and apart from the manifestations of matter.

All these latter doctrines have been incorporated in that philosophical idealism which has dominated European thought in the 2,400 years since his time and remains today as then the irreconcilable adversary of materialism.

XIII. Plato and Aristotle

WITH PLATO AND ARISTOTLE Greek thought attained the peak of its development and became cast into those classical moulds which have been transmitted through the centuries and affect philosophy to our own time. It would be profitable to devote considerable study to these giants of thought. However, most pertinent to this work is their common opposition to materialism as the supreme representatives of idealist thought rather than the not unimportant variations in their individual ideas.

Why did these eminent idealists have such enduring effects upon the course of philosophy in Greece and thereafter?

Idealism first appeared as a coherent view of the world in a society where exchange relations arose out of slave production. But the idealist standpoint reflected the conditions of the slave system far more than the superstructure of market relations. It was the ideological expression of the slaveholding aristocracy in its defensive battle for supremacy against the democratizing tendencies emanating from the mercantile and plebeian forces in the Greek city-states.

The idealists were the first great ideologists of class society and its forms of rule in the Western world. This comes out most clearly in their defense of slavery as ordained by nature, in their championship of the caste system against democracy and of the aristocracy against the claims and aggressions of the people.

An acquaintance with these Greek thinkers is especially useful in correcting the lazy assumption of rationalistic people that all enlightened and educated minds will necessarily arrive at the same general conclusions on social questions. Thanks to the bourgeois-democratic revolutions, it is today a theoretical commonplace that all men are naturally equal and should be brothers in one universal human society. Yet such ideas were utterly alien to these ideologists of the aristocracy in the Greek city-state. They thought the contrary. In their eyes men are by nature unequal and divided into distinct classes. Every one belonged to an appropriate rank in the graded hierarchy of a civic body. Only in that way could men be really human or become thoroughly civilized.

Socrates demonstrated that this was not mere speculation but corresponded to the most deeply held conviction when he refused to flee and submitted to the death penalty imposed upon him by a hostile jury in his native Athens.

The idealists perfected their philosophy in response

to the historical predicament in which the Greek proper-
tied classes of money-lending landowners and slaveholders found themselves toward the close of the 5th
Century. For decades the Greek city-states had been
wracked by class dissensions in which now the oligarchy and now the democracy had the upper hand.

After imperialist expansion brought affluence and
then disaster to the city, the Athenian mercantile and
maritime democracy was close to a dead end. It
could neither help Athens regain its former greatness
nor go further in changing its internal constitution
because of the irremediable antagonism between the
freeman and the slave. This period witnessed the twilight of the first experiment in democratic government.

The idealists elected to defend the oligarchic reaction
against the democratic forces. Plato and Aristotle
both belonged to the patricians; Socrates had close
connections with the same circles. Plato came from a
highly aristocratic family; his uncle Charmides, one
of the personages in his *Dialogues,* was a member of
the directorate of "Thirty" which tried to drown the
democracy in blood.

Diogenes Laertius said of Plato: "In his own country he did not meddle with State affairs, although he
was a politician so far as his writings went. And the
reason was, that the people were accustomed to a
form of government and constitution different from
what he approved of." Completely unsympathetic to
popular rule, Plato dedicated his talents to the justification of ultra-conservatism in his social thought.

However, the petty city-states over which the slave
oligarchy contended were as much on the downgrade

in their day as the democracy they hated. Slavery impoverished and degraded the free citizens. Fourth Century Athens used mercenaries instead of citizens as soldiers, indicating how far the militant democracy of Pericles had deteriorated. In the lifetimes of Plato and Aristotle the Macedonian monarchy was in the process of mastering Greece and overriding the independence of the most powerful of its city-states from Sparta to Athens. This outmoded type of republic was itself about to pass away together with its democracy.

Since the patricians whom they spoke for could only lose from the further unfolding of events, whether that came from a popular movement within their own cities or from military conquest by a foreign power, these philosophers tended to exalt immobility over change in their fundamental ideas and set impassable limits to the historical process.

One of the major tasks of the idealists was to rehabilitate the religious outlook which had fallen into disrepute for many reasons. The clash of moral standards attending the civil and city-state wars had unsettled the old views of the universe along with the positions of its ruling classes. Although they did not deny existence to the gods—even Democritus was still obliged to justify the widespread belief in the gods although he declared that he didn't know what they were like—the criticisms of the materialists, Sophists and other rationalists had considerably discredited the archaic polytheism among the educated classes.

The growing disbelief in the ancient creeds and rituals had to be countered by the reinforcement of religion. The idealist philosophers undertook this by their own elevated methods. They were not the only ones who came to religion's rescue; new popular cults were spreading at the same time among the lower classes. But the philosophers had the special mission of renovating religion for the educated aristocrats.

Thus the Greeks, creators of philosophy, materialism and science, also became the inventors of theology which may be defined as the art of providing rational arguments for religious beliefs. Theology is a branch of apologetics peculiar to commercial civilization; primitive religion does not look for justification from reason nor require it until its foundations have been shaken and its tenets and practices challenged by the enlightened elements of an urban revolution.

The idealist revisions of the nature of the gods arose from political calculations as much as from theoretical considerations. Religion was an indispensable instrument in the technique of aristocratic rule. Religious institutions from the shrine of Apollo at Delphi to the local cults were involved in the stability of oligarchic government, the cohesion of the city-state, the successful prosecution of the struggle for upper-class supremacy, and the subduing of the lower orders. The Delphian Apollo, for example, played a centralizing and conservatizing role in Greek religion and politics like that of the Roman Papacy in medieval times. The neutrality of its priests in the conflict between the Greeks and the Persians had caused many Athenians to doubt the ancestral faith

The value of religion as a social cement and an instrument of class domination was clearly recognized,

candidly discussed and openly acknowledged by the
idealists. Their frankness on this score stands in re-
freshing contrast to the hypocrisy with which modern theologians and politicians seek to conceal the
reactionary influence of religious ideas and institutions. It is highly instructive to study their views because in them can be heard the authentic voice of the
governing class in an aristocratic state.

In *The Republic* Plato disclosed how conscious the
Athenian oligarchs were of the utility of religious doctrines in maintaining class rule by advocating the
application of the "noble lie." After having divided the
inhabitants of his ideal state into the three categories
of Rulers, Auxiliaries and Producers, he discussed
the means by which this social hierarchy could be
perpetuated and the decisions of the Rulers enforced.

Plato asked: " . . . How can we contrive one of
those expedient falsehoods we were speaking of just
now, one noble falsehood, which we may persuade
the whole community, including the Rulers, themselves, if possible, to accept?"

He answered that it would be best to present the
formation of this class-divided society as an old
Phoenician story, that is, invest its origins with an
aura of antiquity to place it beyond immediate investigation and easy checkup. Then he goes on to say:
"We shall tell them that all of you are brothers; but,
when God was fashioning those of you who are fit
to rule, he mixed in some gold, so these are the most
valuable; and he put silver in the Auxiliaries, and
iron and bronze in the farmers and other craftsmen.
Since you are all akin, your children will mostly be

like their parents, but occasionally a golden parent may have a silver child or a silver parent a golden child, and so on; and therefore the first and foremost task that God has laid upon the Rulers is, of all their functions as Guardians, to pay the most careful attention to the mixture of metals in the souls of children, so that, if one of their own children is born with an alloy of iron or bronze, they must not give way to pity but cast it out among the craftsmen and farmers, thus assigning it to the station appropriate to its nature; and conversely, if one of these should produce a child with silver or gold in it, they must promote him to the Guardians or Auxiliaries, according to his value, in the belief that it has been foretold that, if ever the state should fall into the keeping of a bronze and iron guardian, it will be ruined. That is the story. Can you suggest any device by which we can get them to believe it?"

" . . . Not the first generation, but perhaps their sons and descendants and eventually the whole posterity," came the reply.

In this passage the connection between religious fables and the techniques of class domination is exposed to full view. To justify the caste system of Plato's *Republic,* the citizens are to be duped into believing the noble lies that God created social distinctions, that differences in social status arose from inborn differences in the makeup of men and indeed from the very nature of things, and that if those of baser metal should capture power, the divine order of excellence would be overturned and the Republic ruined. It is interesting, by the way, to observe how the caste system is described in terms of the precious metals which are the core of a monetary economy.

Plato was not the only one, then or since, to point out the political value of the noble lie in upholding social inequality. But he is certainly one of the most direct exponents of its necessity. Others who have found it indispensable in practice have feared to justify its use so explicitly in theoretical terms.

The Greek idealists completed the task of rationalizing the outworn people's religion by replacing mythology with theology, although neither Socrates nor Plato entirely dispensed with myths. Whenever they ran into difficulties in the exposition of their idealism, they resorted to myths to eke out their lack of argument and positive knowledge. This was a common practice among Greek thinkers. For example, Plato used an allegory to account for the history of the soul before joining the body and after leaving it and invoked the legend of Atlantis to explain the prehistory of mankind.

The idealist philosophers transformed the substance of religion and gave it a new dress. They applied the new logical and dialectical techniques which in themselves were precious innovations to shore up the shaken superstitions.

We have already seen how Socrates viewed mankind as the handiwork of God and the rest of the universe as contrived by a benevolent Providence for our welfare. That is one side of the matter. But the divine was also identified with the patriarchal slavemasters. "The nature of the divine is to rule and direct, and that of the mortal to be subject and serve," he says in the *Phaedo*. "The gods are our keepers, and we men are one of their possessions." Moreover, the Gods are the very best of masters whose dictates ought not be questioned.

Plato set forth a similar conception. For him the universe is a beautiful work of art created by a Supreme Intelligence according to a premeditated design for the good of mankind. The world itself has a living soul created by God, just as men have a living soul which is the seat of intelligence.

Aristotle, who gave theology its name, regarded it as the highest of the sciences. He identified it with knowledge of that kind of being which combines substantial, self-dependent existence with freedom from all change. In his system of ideas the divine is the immortal, the unchangeable, the ultimate source of motion which is itself unmoved and unmovable.

In his book on *Metaphysics* Aristotle argues that there must be an eternal substance which causes eternal circular motion and to be everlasting this substance must be immaterial. There must be something which moves the starry heavens without itself being moved. This unmoved mover is God who directly sets the stars in motion by inspiring love and desire in their souls. All other things derive their movements from the same prime mover. This prime mover is knowledge which has only itself for its object. God's sole activity is that of knowing.

By a host of similar arguments in their works Plato and Aristotle sought to transmute mythology into theology by way of teleology. The supreme service they rendered to religion and the ruling classes since their day is to have made the supernatural more acceptable to the critical intelligence by assigning logical reasons for its alleged existence and activities.

Their logic was far from impeccable. Although Aristotle's God, for example, knows nothing but himself and moves all things, he explicitly denies that God has any knowledge of evil. His God does not create material substance which is eternal; He is an immaterial being who moves it. These contradictions in his conception of God, or rather limitations upon the divine power and attributes, were to cause considerable trouble to the Arabian and Christian theologians who relied upon his views.

Christian theology plundered Plato and Aristotle and is deeply indebted to them. No small measure of their prestige and sustained influence as a philosophical tendency is due to their theological and teleological doctrines which have proved enormously helpful to many ideologists of the upper classes since.

As philosophical representatives of the Greek aristocrats, the idealists elaborated their characteristic views in direct and conscious opposition to the ideas advanced by materialistically inclined spokesmen. We have previously discussed how Socrates turned away from Anaxagoras on the ground that he failed to accord *Nous.* or Intelligence, the critical role in explaining phenomena and thereafter sought for signs of the divine reason to indicate that everything everywhere was for the best. In the same passage Socrates rejects Empedocles, Anaximenes, and Democritus because they look for the causes of things in such material phenomena as the vortex or air rather than in what is really good and fitting. The task of the philosopher, he says, is to show that nature, and the nature of everything, accords with some rational end contrived by divine purpose.

Plato was an even more implacable opponent of the materialists. In *The Phaedo,* which sets forth his arguments for the immortality of the soul, he rejects theories put forward by Simmias and Cebes that would make the soul dependent upon the laws of physical change and decay. Simmias argues that the soul may be likened to the attunement of the lyre and that just as the attunement vanishes when the lyre is broken and the strings severed, so the soul perishes when the body is dead.

Plato through Socrates disposes of these materialist objections by denying that the soul can be compared to an attunement because attunement is a matter of degree whereas the soul is fixed and unvarying and because an attunement cannot be at discord with the elements composing it whereas the soul lords it over the passions and emotions of the body.

Plato directly alluded to his irreconcilable struggle against the materialists in setting forth the doctrine of the Ideal Forms which constituted his theory of knowledge and depended upon the acknowledgement of the immortal soul. In *The Sophist* he wrote: — "Why, this dispute about reality is a sort of Battle of Gods and Giants. One side drags everything down to earth, literally laying hands on rocks and trees, arguing that only what can be felt and touched is real, defining reality as body, and if anyone says that something

without body is real, they treat him with contempt
and will not listen to another word.

"—Yes, they are clever fellows; I've met a lot of
them.

"—So their opponents in the height of the unseen
defend their position with great skill, maintaining
forcibly that true existence consists in certain intelligible, incorporeal forms, describing the so-called truth
of the others as a mere flowing sort of becoming,
not reality at all, and smashing their so-called bodies
to pieces. On this issue there is a terrific battle always
going on."

As George Thomson points out in Volume II of
his *Studies in Ancient Greek Society,* the Giants are
the materialists and the Gods are the idealists.

In *The Laws* Plato condemns the materialists as
godless men who undermine religion, subvert the existing moral order, foment civil strife, mislead the
young and corrupt their morals.

"—They say that earth, air, fire and water all exist
by nature or chance, not by art, and that by means
of these wholly inanimate substances there have come
into being the secondary bodies—the earth, sun, moon
and stars. Set in motion by their individual properties and mutual affinities, such as hot and cold, wet
and dry, hard and soft, and all the other combinations formed by necessity from the chance admixture
of opposites—in this way heaven has been created and
everything that is in it, together with all the animals
and plants, and the seasons too are of the same origin—not by means of mind or God or art but, as I
said, by nature and chance. Art arose after these and

out of them, mortal in origin, producing certain toys which do not really partake of truth but consist of related images, such as those produced by painting, music and the accompanying arts, while the arts which do have some serious purpose, co-operate actively with nature, such as medicine, agriculture and gymnastics; and so does politics too to some extent, but it is mostly art; and so with legislation—it is entirely art, not nature, and its assumptions are not true.

"—How do you mean?

"—The Gods, my friend, according to these people, have no existence in nature but only in art, being a product of laws, which differ from place to place according to the conventions of the lawgivers; and natural goodness is different from what is good by law; and there is no such thing as natural justice; they are constantly discussing it and changing it; and, since it is a matter of art and law and not of nature, whatever changes they make in it from time to time are valid for the moment. This is what our young people hear from professional poets and private persons, who assert that might is right; and the result is, they fall into sin, believing that the gods are not what the law bids them imagine them to be, and into civil strife, being induced to live according to nature, that is, by exercising actual dominion over others instead of living in legal subjection to them.

"—What a dreadful story, and what an outrage to the public and private morals of the young!"

These tunes are familiar; they sound like the accusations against the materialists and Marxists coming from conservative circles today.

Aristotle was the first historian of philosophy and explicitly developed his own ideas in constant critical comparison with those of his predecessors. He refuted previous opinions and exposed the errors and shortcomings of the earlier materialists in order to validate his own positions. Indeed, many of his criticisms of specific views of the earlier materialists were quite warranted and well-founded.

But Aristotle carefully counterposed his own ideas to those of the materialists in his conceptions of nature, society and the thought processes. His idealism is particularly pronounced in his conception of what nature is. Whereas the physicists regarded nature as wholly material, Aristotle saw nature as a mixture of matter and form, or end and purpose. Natural events unfold like human art. They are all animated by thought and directed toward a specific end which realizes its essential character and implicit aim. Nothing in nature is done in vain or without purpose. All perishable things aspire in their movements to the Good and the Perfect, more or less clearly desired, which is God, the unmoved mover, the thought of thought.

This formidable phalanx of idealist philosophers gave battle to the materialists and overwhelmed them, or at least placed them thereafter on the defensive. The idealists were assisted in their onslaught not only by their association with the material interests of the ruling oligarchy but also by certain inescapable weaknesses in the arsenal of their philosophical adversaries.

The early materialists gave cogent explanations of the origins and operations of natural phenomena and of the beginnings and development of society. They displayed astonishing insight for their time in analyzing the central points in these two spheres of reality.

But the first materialists were weak and vulnerable when it came to accounting for the invisible but extremely important phenomena bound up with the mental processes. The idealists, on the other hand, proved exceptionally able in this field of science. The idealists were experts in the examination of the thought processes and masters in the handling of general conceptions. They advanced and clarified the problems of knowing while the materialists contributed most to the problems of being and becoming. The outstanding idealists from Pythagoras to Plato rejected the premises of primitive materialism, among other reasons, because these did not deal adequately with the origins, nature, functions and properties of ideas and did not properly analyze and appreciate the generalizing capacities of the human reason, especially in mathematics. The classical Greek idealists held a fundamentally false philosophical position but they were keen enough to detect the flaws in their opponents! And it was to take a long time before this defect in materialism was to be removed.

XIV. Achievements of the Idealists

ONE OF THE PREREQUISITES for the rise of philosophy was the existence of leisured people who were relieved of unremitting toil by slaves and given the time and means to devote themselves to theoretical discussion and inquiry. Plato's theory that rulers should be philosophers and the philosophers rulers in the ideal Republic, and Aristotle's conception of God as pure thought thinking about itself, are projections of this state of affairs.

But the same situation which assigned the labors of material production to bondsmen and the tasks of theorizing and rulership to an aristocracy in need of justifying itself impressed its stamp upon the course and results of all its reasoning. The idealists introduced sharp divisions into reality. They exalted pure reason above practice, the mind above the senses and appetites, the soul above the body, and God above man. They elevated the masters above the masses

226

and evolved theories which sanctioned social inequality in its grossest forms, the subordination of slaves to owners, non-citizens to citizens, women to men and barbarians to Greeks. Their science subserved theology and both served the political aims and material interests of the slaveholders.

The structure of Greek idealist thought corresponded in essentials with the hierarchical structure of the slave system. The master-slave relationship dominated their views of nature, society and the individual; its influence is marked not only in ethics and politics but in their physical theories, physiology and psychology.

In Plato's *Republic* all intelligence, all power, all will are concentrated in the golden men, the fully enlightened master class, while "the lesser breed" made of baser metal is congenitally incapable of reason, command or self-rule.

The soul itself consists of three parts: the reason, the spirit and the appetites. The reason corresponds to the rulers, the spirit to the guardians or police, the appetites to the workers.

The body is conceived on the same pattern. The head is separated from the trunk by the neck because the divine part of the soul, located in the head, must be saved from pollution by the menial part lower down.

Mind and matter are opposed to each other like master and slave. Matter is inherently disorderly and unruly, and whatever regularity and beauty exists in nature comes from mind which imposes order upon it.

The Ionian natural philosophers had interpreted the material world as evolving in accord with its internal laws. In Aristotle's scheme of nature, matter is the refractory element which causes disorder and disruption while various types of rational causes directed this otherwise recalcitrant element toward specific ends. As Farrington points out [*Greek Science, p. 146*], mind is thus made to resemble a master which has ends at which it aims and imposes its will upon matter. Matter sometimes resists those ends and, like the slave, can achieve nothing except under the direction of a superior will. Matter and the slave were equally degraded and servile.

The same hidden social impulses led the idealists to exalt reasoning above sense evidence, detach theory from practice and oppose the two in principle. For them the exaltation of the one involved the degradation of the other. The philosopher-king who contemplates ideal reality by means of pure reason and is thereby in communion with the Good, the Beautiful and the Divine is set apart and above the ordinary mortals of the workaday world who are craftsmen, technicians, practitioners of the arts. Their detachment from the spheres of material production induces the idealists to low-rate the techniques of production involved in the alterations of matter.

In the *Symposium* Plato says that the man who is wise in the knowledge of love that mediates between gods and men is a semi-divine being; the man who is only wise in arts and handicrafts is vulgar. Plato draws a sharp distinction between such studies as music, gymnastics, mathematics, astronomy and dialectics which are gentlemanly and excellent, fitting for the superior orders, and the crafts which are vulgar and menial, dulling the mind, crippling the body, and proper to the lower nature and portions of mankind.

Aristotle apologizes for speaking of mechanics and other practical operations, saying that they are rightly despised by wise men and philosophers. Plato even devalues the use of mathematical demonstrations into which mechanics was introduced. He declared that geometry was corrupted and robbed of its dignity by making it go "like a runaway slave from the study of the incorporeal, intelligible things to that of objects which come under the senses and by using, in addition to reasoning, bodies which have been fashioned, slowly and slavishly, by manual labor."

Xenophon, his disciple, said: "The crafts called menial give a man no opportunity to devote himself to his friends or to the city; so that men of this sort seem incompetent to benefit friends and defend their country. So that in some states, and particularly those that seem to be the best governed, no citizen may engage in menial tasks." Xenophon was referring to conservative Sparta and archaic Crete.

This disdain for manual activities coupled with an overestimation of pure intellectual operations divorced from practical application has remained a hallmark of the theoretical outlook of the upper classes from that day to this. It may be seen nowadays, for example, in the contention that philosophy has, or should have, no direct connection with politics and is of no concern or use to the working masses.

The consummate expression of this attitude is contained in the Platonic conception of eternal Ideas or perfect Forms which is the essence of his idealist theory of being and of knowledge. Plato's theory of knowledge resulted from a twofold transformation of real things and their mental reflections. On the one side, he took material things and transformed them into their ideas; on the other side he took the ideas of things and converted them into the essential reality of the things themselves.

How did he perform this act of transubstantiation which was as miraculous and mystifying as the changing of the wafer and the wine of the Catholic sacrement into the body and blood of Christ—and belonged to the same order of theorizing?

The earlier "physical" philosophers had looked for the permanence of things in matter or in one of the material elements. Heraclitus had pointed out that all things were in flux and subject to constant change through the opposing forces at work within them. The Sophists had insisted on the changeability and conventionality of social customs, political institutions and moral codes.

Plato developed his theory of eternal ideas in outright opposition to all these tendencies, offering it as a solution to the problems they had raised. He admitted that physical phenomena are always changing and entangled in contradictions. Their appearances represent an incessant succession of contraries in which it is impossible to hold fast to anything permanent. But this changeability and these manifold, elusive, contradictory properties belong only to empirical things, to matter, to the bodily state, to sense perception.

There is another and higher grade of existence which is represented and reflected within the ever-changing physical phenomena. These are the Ideas or Forms. They constitute the essential reality, the permanent identity in things and their appearances. The Forms are not subject to any inner opposition. They are forever identical with themselves, motionless, uniform, ungenerable and incorruptible. They are totally independent of the flux of things and intrinsically fixed and stable.

Let us take two examples from Plato of such eternal Ideas or Forms. Something is wet. What is wet? Wetness is a physical property, caused, as we now know, by the presence of water or some similar chemical compound in the body. But not for Plato. For him a body is wet or becomes so, by participating in, or springing from the Idea or Form of Wetness. The wetness of any particular thing may become less or more, or disappear entirely but Wetness does not increase, diminish or perish. Its existence is eternal; its nature is unchangeable. Ordinary, palpable wetness is a copy of this immortal idea.

The same contrast applies to social relations such as virtue, justice, love, friendship, etc., as to physical properties like wetness. There are many virtues, says Plato. But they acquire excellence because each of these particular goodnesses shares in the Idea or Form of virtue as such. virtue is the common essence of which the many virtues partake, endowing them with the special quality of virtue, just as the gold of the ingot causes all its parts to be golden.

As materialists, we know that there is no real gold

apart from the metallic substance which is the material reality. To be sure, in addition to this physically existent metal and its social fabrications into ornaments, money, etc., there has arisen the general conception of gold in our minds. But this idea of gold, or formal scientific definition of goldness, is no more than an abstraction from real gold. It is not an eternal Form more real than all the samples of the metal in the objective world which gave birth to this conceptual generalization.

Plato, however, thought and taught otherwise. The Idea or Form in our mind of wetness, straightness, evenness and any other physical property and relation, or virtue, goodness, justice and other social phenomena or moral values, was infinitely more permanent, more real, more true, more essential than any of its empirical manifestations or material copies.

For him the process of learning about reality consisted in progressing from pure ignorance through opinion to absolute knowledge. These stages of knowing corresponded to correlative grades of being: non-being, phenomena, and perfect being, as well as to correlative means of cognition from the sensation to the intellect. There was a precise parallelism between every grade of being and every stage of knowing. Sense perception shows things in their contradictions, as both one and many at the same time, as wet and dry, cold and hot. But then the intellect steps in, disentangles these contradictions, and introduces unity and order into the flux of contradictory appearances by singling out the eternal ideas within them.

The pure Forms are completely immaterial and

accessible to pure thought only. These supreme entities are enthroned in a higher realm far above the mundane welter of things. Plato regarded the objects of mathematics and of moral values as the finest examples of these eternal Ideas, although his Ideal doctrine extended over all things.

Where did these pure Forms come from? They were not derived from memories or generalizations from everyday sense experiences, although these evoked them. They had a different origin. They came from a previous life; men recollected them. Their discovery, or rather recovery, pointed to the existence of a higher and better world in the after-life provided they were consistently pursued in this one. The philosopher is one who does not permit himself to be beguiled by the transient appearances of things but seeks and cherishes their rational essence. Why?

The Forms are the causes of all phenomena. They make things what they are. Wetness makes things wet; Justice makes men and their actions good. The ultimate cause of all things, the Form of Forms, is the Form of the Good. Everything partakes of the Good and it is necessary to look for the Goodness in all things to uncover its cause or logical reason for being. The greatest Good available to men is to use their reason to discover this divine Goodness in all things.

This Platonic doctrine of eternal Ideas or Forms as causes serves an indispensable function in the idealist scheme of things. It becomes the rational basis for the recognition of absolute ideas and the establishment of timeless standards which are immune to change. Not being man-made, they cannot—or should not—be questioned, assaulted or replaced by human action. This enabled the idealists to assert that everything has to be measured in comparison with absolute standards. These were the basis of all order in the universe, society and the individual. They were unchanging and divinely inspired; they regulated and checked chaos in nature and the state, just as the reason which recognized them curbed the appetites within the individual. They guaranteed that the best had the right to rule and that the justice they dispensed was immovably grounded in eternal verities.

The idealists interpreted absolute standards in accord with the outlook of the Athenian aristocracy; their concrete content was derived from the essential requirements of that ruling class. The voice of the slaveholder is plainly heard when Socrates says in the *Phaedo* that suicide is wrong because God is our keeper and we are his possessions; it would be as foolish to quit the body before God's will in the hope of a better life as it would be for a slave to run away from a good master.

The same bent is discernible in such seemingly remote ranges of Plato's thought as his astronomical theories. He asserted that planets must move in circular and uniform motion because irregularity was incompatible with the procedure of a gentleman. And he expressed dismay over the erratic behavior of the planets and meteors which were vagabonds in the otherwise orderly sky.

The slaveholding bias is no less evident in Plato's doctrine of the soul that man is subject to God and the body to the soul as the slave is to his master. Such is the eternal nature of things which it is the highest wisdom to acknowledge in theory and obey in practical life. From top to bottom the idealist philosophy is shaped and stigmatized by this class relation of domination and subservience which is supposedly ordained by nature and divinely decreed.

Idealism is likewise marred by an incurable dualism from one end to the other. Its two opposite ends never meet in reality. There remains an impassable gulf between perishable phenomena and timeless Forms; between body and soul; between theory and practice; between God and man; between master and slave. These are to be kept strictly apart because they belong to wholly separate realms. To mix them up or confuse them is the fruit of ignorance, the source of disorder, the cause of anarchy.

Two essentially different worlds confront each other with no passageway open between them. This ineradicable dualism is characteristic of the ideological world-outlook of ruling classes which must, in order to protect and perpetuate their privileged positions, erect impassable barriers at some point around them. Thus the universe is split into the unchanging heavens and the ever-changing earth; nature into degraded matter and divine Forms; material things into copies and essences; society into masters and servants; the human being into a pure immortal soul and an earthly corruptible body. This cleavage in the highest domains of theory reflected the insuperable cleavage within slaveholding society.

This situation is pictured by Plato in his parable of

the cave. Mankind is held prisoner by the body as in a cave. In this life we are seated facing the back wall of the cave and see shadowy outlines passing along it as though on a screen. These are projections of the pure Forms passing back and forth before the entrance to the cave which the sun casts upon the wall before us. The passing procession of reflections of the eternal Ideas are the things we see all about us in the sublunary sensory world.

The philosopher is one who understands the shadowy, unsubstantial nature of these mere material manifestations and sees the divine reality of the ideal realm in these perishable copies.

This is a beautiful image—but it reverses the real relations between material reality and its reflections in our mind. The objective world which exists outside of us is the primary reality and the ideas are derived multiform reflections of its diverse aspects in our minds.

Aristotle made many modifications in Plato's view of the world and especially in his theory of Ideas. In place of the Forms as the sole causes of things, he introduced the doctrine of the fourfold causes; material, efficient, formal and final.

Aristotle's chief criticism of the materialists was that they recognized only one kind of cause in their explanations of the becoming and being of things, the material cause. They did not go beyond asking: out of what does something come and out of what is it made?

Three other kinds of causes, or reasons, must be taken into account in order to understand any process, says Aristotle. It must be asked: what is it? This is the formal cause. Through what agency did it occur? This is the efficient cause. Last but most important, for what end does it come into existence? This is the final cause.

All of these causes cooperate in generating every existing thing in the universe and the universe itself. In order to render anything intelligible, all four necessary conditions of existence have to be analyzed.

However, the decisive cause of existence is not the material but the final cause. This is the end which realizes the Idea of the thing in actuality and in which its Form is most fully expressed. In Aristotle's system nature is essentially teleological because everything comes into existence and develops in order to fulfill its own specific end.

This teleological conception of universal causation in which God, the supreme being, the Form of Forms, the absolute end, is the ultimate cause of all lower grades of being, gives Aristotle's physics and metaphysics its anti-materialist character.

Aristotle did not dissociate matter from form, the particular from the general, or things from ideas as sharply as Plato did. He modified the theory of Ideas as causes to bring it closer to material reality and diminish the distance between existing things and their ideal causes. But in the last analysis Aristotle, too, falls back upon the final cause in the shape of the Idea as the basic cause of all things and must therefore be classed with the idealist school. For example, although he regards matter and form as inseparable and interchangeable, the form is the dynamic factor which makes things what they must be. Throughout nature form strives to realize itself against the obstructive resistance of the matter.

To all the idealists from Socrates to Aristotle, thought, reason, the general idea, the Form was primary and predominant in generating and explaining the nature of reality. Material formations themselves were only receptacles for the ideas which were revealed by reason and ultimately owed their features, functions and powers to the Supreme Reason or Reasoner who was divine.

This is the essence of idealism. Idealism, like materialism, has changed its form and dress and modified its substance many times over the past 2,500 years. But its basic ideas have remained the same as they were cast by the Greek thinkers of the 4th Century B.C. All subsequent schools of idealist philosophy are descended from these classical Greeks. This community of thought extends from the Christian Saint Augustine, Plotinus and the medieval theologians to the principal doctrines of the illustrious idealists of the 17th, 18th and 19th Centuries from the German Leibnitz through the English Bishop Berkeley to Hegel, the last of the great idealist thinkers.

It likewise embraces their contemporary descendants who dominate official philosophy in the universities. The difference is that the idealist titans of antiquity and the early bourgeois epoch contributed many valuable elements to the advancement of knowledge which have been incorporated into the permanent treasury of philosophic thought whereas today's pigmies repeat old errors which hold back the progress of philosophy.

▣ The Contributions of Greek Idealism
to Philosophy

THE GREAT IDEALIST philosophers were thoroughgoing rationalists both in method and in practice. There is a difference between rationalism and idealism. Rationalism insists that everything must have a sufficient cause and every concept must submit itself to the tests of reasonable criticism. In this sense, rationalism goes beyond idealism and is incorporated into the method of any mature materialist philosophy as well.

The classical idealists demanded that everything justify itself in the light of methodical reasoning. They did not depend upon tradition, revelation, intuition, mysticism or any other irrational faculty for the discovery and demonstration of what was real, true, good or beautiful. They relied exclusively upon the activities of the intelligence and its methods. The spirit of their rationalism was expressed in Socrates' dictum that "the unexamined life is not worth living." Socrates argued against any distrust of reasoning and constantly urged his interlocutors to bring forward their doubts, criticisms and objections, not in order to counterpose his views to theirs dogmatically, but in order to improve and extend their mutual understanding and thereby round out and perfect one-sided or superficial views.

The idealists rationalized religion and ideologically justified the interests of the slaveholding oligarchy.

239

But they did much more than that. They gave a theoretical basis to many branches of knowledge for the first time: economics, politics, mathematics, morality, aesthetics, logic, biology, etc.

Idealism has its historical source in class society where a minority which owns and controls the conditions of labor compels the majority to carry out its orders. So long as intellectual labor is separated from manual labor and the superintendence of production from the tasks of material production, the favored few devoted to scientific and theoretical pursuits can easily fall victim to the illusion that ideas can be independent of things. Idealism erects this alleged primacy of theory over practice and pure reason over sensory experience into the governing principle of the universe.

But idealism is not simply the result of the division of labor in a commodity-producing society. It is the outgrowth of the process of knowledge itself, or rather, of its unwitting abuse.

The instrument of knowledge is the concept. Concepts are generalizations from experiences of things arrived at by abstraction. They have a dual character. While concepts reflect or formulate features of their object, they do so in a partial manner. Even the most correct and comprehensive concepts cannot help but distort the realities dealt with to some extent since they express the contents and connections of things only relatively and approximately, not absolutely and wholly.

Idealism disconnects the products of abstraction from the real conditions they represent. It isolates one aspect of knowledge from the whole—in the case of the Greeks, ideas—and then tries to force all of reality into this single arbitrary mould.

Purposiveness, for example, is operative in human action and its concept is applicable to the analysis of human motives. But idealism illegitimately extends this concept to cover nature and the historical process as a whole where it is out of place. Or, it makes reason, which is the product of nature and society, into their creator.

Although materialist thinking may often in practice be tripped up by the inherent tendency of conceptual reflection to diverge from reality and deform it, it has built in safeguards by its demand that ideas correspond to objective realities. This keeps a tighter rein upon the vices of abstraction and restrains thought from wandering beyond the bounds of real existence.

Dialectical thinking consciously counteracts and overcomes this shortcoming of the thought process in two ways: first, by combining individual concepts according to the laws of the movement of their objects and second, by submitting the conclusions of theory to the continual tests of practice.

Uninhibited by these materialist considerations, the idealists press abstraction to the point where they end up with fantastic deformations of reality and with ideas that are completely arbitrary, empty and false. Thus, in their extremely lopsided version of reality, the Greeks extracted one side of human experience, its ideological activities, and carried it to extremes. They excessively exaggerated the place and power of thought in the development of the universe, the history of society and the life of mankind.

But this very concentration upon the mind induced the outstanding idealists to pay special attention to its processes and study its peculiar features very closely. They are responsible for many brilliant scientific insights into the forms and laws of thought.

Since its origins, mankind had engaged in thinking to one degree or another. But *systematic* thought covering definite domains of knowledge, and especially systematic thought about thought itself, was a new and mighty power in society. It could not be known in advance of experiment and observation of its results just what the special properties and functions of thought were and what were their limits. Indeed, these have still to be determined. Its capacities had to be discovered through practice, by trial and error, by pressing the exercise of thought not only to its limits but beyond them. Often, in scientific work, in the progress of thought, nothing succeeds like excess. In the discovery of what is excessive, that is, beyond the bounds of material reality, social necessity and logical possibility, the indispensable corrections which lead to truth can be made.

This was one of the historical services of idealism. By pushing thought beyond its permissible material limits, the idealists helped discover the powers and define the essential province and properties of intelligence.

After all, consider how little the baby knows about its body. In the course of growing up, the child not only discovers that it has a separate body but also what the functions of its various organs are and how they are interconnected.

Even today, physiological, biochemical and medical research is discovering many new things about the body from the functions of the endocrine and other glands to its methods of stabilization after stress. In Greek times, the first scientists had still to find out some of the most elementary things about the human body including the circulation of the blood and the function of the nervous system.

In the first flush of innovation, the idealists inevitably entertained many wrong and exaggerated notions about the mental processes which are still more difficult to examine and explore. The wonder is not that they went wrong in so many ways but that they were right in so many.

The Greeks were not the first to reason. But they were the first to reason about reasoning, to try and find the rules of the thought processes, to formulate and systematize the modes of thought. They were the inventors of logic, the science of the thought process.

Socrates invented definition and adduction. Plato made the first attempts to define the categories of thought, such as being, quantity, quality and relation. He tried to find out what judgment was and what made it valid, what relation the particular had to the general.

Even though he used it to support conclusions that the ideas are eternal and above material reality, Plato's theory of Ideas aimed to apply a critical method to reality in order to make it intelligible to the intelligence. For example, in the *Parmenides,*

Plato takes such correlative pairs of ideas as the one and the many, being and not-being, likeness and unlikeness, movement and rest, generation and corruption and then tries to see what logical consequences follow when they are dialectically treated. He first examines each one of the pair in respect to itself, then in relation to its opposite, and then does the same for its own opposite. In this way he derives two positions and eight consequences for each idea.

This dialectical method, further corrected and much amplified, became a starting point and basis for the dialectical logic of Hegel. This in turn, materialistically based and historically interpreted and applied, became an indispensable part of dialectical materialism. Thus the valid results of the logical researches of the idealists entered into the heritage of modern materialism.

Aristotle set forth in his writings the first fully developed system of logic which summed up the achievements of the idealists in this field. He collected, classified, codified, criticized and systematized all the positive results of thinking about the thought processes which the Greeks investigated. His formal logic was the first system of the scientific knowledge of the thought processes and is one of the crowning glories of Greek thought.

The idealist philosophers made many other important contributions to the natural sciences from biology and botany to zoology. They fostered the study of mathematics and especially geometry. Over the entrance to Plato's academy there was supposedly inscribed the injunction: "Let none who cannot geometrize enter here." His disciple, Eudoxus, studied the theory of proportions and invented the method of exhaustion which consisted in bringing two unequal sizes or quantities ever closer together by exhausting or diminishing their differences.

Aristotle and his school brought biology to a point that was not to be surpassed until modern times. His psychological observations were not superseded until the 19th Century. The idealists made exceptionally valuable contributions to the social and cultural sciences. They were the originators of the sciences of economics, politics, of the criticism of morality, aesthetics, etc.

The first scientific discoveries in astronomy and mathematics had been made by the priestly scribes and temple administrators of Babylonia and Egypt. The philosopher-scientists of Ionia escaped from this priestly tradition. The idealists carried forward sustained collective intellectual activity a step further by making their scientific and philosophical work an organized cooperative effort free of clerical control. The Platonic Academy endured 700 years; Aristotle's Lyceum had a much shorter life but during it his successor Theophrastus and others made considerable contributions to science and education.

The idealists from Socrates to Aristotle demonstrated how to analyze the most general forms of nature, society and human thought and distinguish the essential from the non-essential in all the phenomena they studied. This remains a necessity for all genuinely scientific knowledge, despite the errors which the idealists fell into.

Finally, the idealists made memorable contributions

to literature and to the art of living. Socrates was the personification of the unresting critic, probing beneath surfaces for the truth of things. Plato was the master of philosophical dialogue. Aristotle was the greatest thinker of antiquity.

There were distinct differences among this trio in the degree of their idealism. In Socrates idealism is still in its formative stage; in Plato it is completely crystallized. He is the supreme representative of the idealist outlook in his age as Leibnitz and Hegel were in the bourgeois era. Aristotle's philosophical studies, as Thomson remarks [*Studies In Ancient Greek Society*, Vol. I., p. 330], reveal a gradual though incomplete emancipation from unalloyed idealism. He was unable to throw off its limitations because of his aversion to practical techniques in theory and his subservience to the needs of the slave system.

Thus we are indebted to the classical idealists for many precious discoveries which give them an imperishable place in human thought.*

---

* These aspects of the work of the idealists are not always correctly appreciated by empiricists or narrow-minded materialists. For instance, in his book on historical materialism, Bukharin designated Plato as a man of outspoken "Black Hundred" tendencies, that is, the equivalent of a fascist. It is undeniable that Plato expressed the views of a slaveholding ruling class. But so, for that matter, did Washington and Jefferson in their time and in their way. If there was no more enduring substance to Plato's thought than that, he would hardly have exerted the immense influence he has through the centuries. But that is only one side of his output.

This disparagement of the work and worth of the great Greek idealists can be found in others who embrace Marxism. In his otherwise sound book on **Greek Science** Farrington correctly contrasts the idealism of Socrates toward nature unfavorably with the Ionian thinkers who offered a materialist explanation of nature and man. But then he adds: "It is likely that he made important contributions to logic. Aristotle credits him with introducing Induction and Definition. But . . . he made no contribution to science."

It would have to be concluded from these remarks either that logic was not a science or that science had no need for logic. However, if Socrates created several basic elements of logic, as he very likely did, then he certainly made indispensable contributions to the science of logic, if not to the logic of science.

In fact, Farrington here displays too narrow a view of science, an inadequate appreciation of the history and value of logic, and therewith an inadequate appraisal of Socrates and the other master logicians of the Greek idealist tradition.

XV. The Philosophy of Epicurus

THE LINE OF MATERIALIST philosophy which had been started by the Ionians and developed into Atomism by Leucippus and Democritus was perfected by Epicurus and his school. Epicurus lived from 341 to 268 B.C. His life span extended from six years after Plato's death to fifty-five years after the deaths of Aristotle and Alexander the Great.

He was born of Athenian parents on the island of Samos, and, after a period of military service in the Athenian army, taught philosophy in several centers until he founded his famous Garden School at Athens where he lived and taught his disciples in the last twenty years of his life.

The reputation of Epicureanism has come down to our own time in two senses. In popular speech it is equated with sensualism, deliberate indulgence in coarse pleasures, submergence in bodily appetites. An epicure is a person fond of foods, wines, etc. This would more properly apply to the school of hedonism founded by Aristippus at Cyrene than to the doctrines of the historical Epicurus. It is a reverberation of the anti-materialist slander of a materialist school.

In its other guise Epicureanism is identified with atheism. The hatred of orthodox Jews for the heretical teachings of Epicurus is recorded in the rabbinical term for apostate: *Apikoras* (Epicurean). This, too, is a half-truth. The Epicureans, as materialists, did not believe either in a pre-life or an after-life, in the immortality of the soul or the omnipotence of a benevolent and just God. However, they were not atheists. They taught that gods existed but lived in the spaces between worlds, occupied with themselves and not bothering about the affairs of men. But this removal of divinity from our world was enough to stamp them as disbelievers in the eyes of Jews and Christians.

Epicurus was a learned man familiar with the entire preceding course of Greek thought; he based his philosophy upon the atomism of Leucippus and Democritus. But he came to atomic materialism after it had been subjected to criticism by the classical idealists and was obliged to revise the atomistic positions in the light of these criticisms as well as in line with the sweeping changes in Greek life during his career.

His reconstruction of atomism began with accepting its essential positions which he codified in twelve elementary principles.

1. Matter is uncreatable.
2. Matter is indestructible.
3. The universe consists of solid bodies and void.
4. Solid bodies are either compounds or simple.

5. The multitude of atoms is infinite.

6. The void is infinite in extent.

7. The atoms are always in motion.

8. The speed of atomic motion is uniform.

9. Motion is linear in space, vibratory in compounds.

10. Atoms are capable of swerving slightly at any point in space and time.

11. Atoms are characterized by three qualities: weight, shape and size.

12. The number of the different shapes is not infinite, merely innumerable.

In these propositions Epicurus systematized the physical foundations of the materialist view of the world devised by his forerunners. Unlike Democritus, he gave the atoms an essential weight so that they moved downward and said that their shapes were finite. But the principal point on which he diverged from his predecessors in physical theory was his hypothesis of an infinitely small but spontaneous swerve from the vertical line of descent. Democritus had left no room for chance in his cosmology, no place for accident in sociology and choice in morality. In his scheme of the universe the atoms fell vertically through empty space, creating the world and all things in it by their collisions and combinations. He thus outlined a rigidly deterministic theory of the universe in which every event is the product of strict necessity and nothing happens by chance in the world or by choice in human life.

Epicurus introduced a deviation from the perpendicular into the very nature of the atoms and their downward motion. This served two purposes. First, in physics it made possible the entanglement of the atoms which would otherwise fall in parallel lines and never meet to form compound bodies; he regarded this as a defect of the Democritean physics. Second, in morality it liberated mankind from subjection to an infinite and inescapable chain of physical causation and made freedom of choice possible.

The reasons for this innovation were not solely of a theoretical character but were rooted in the changed historical situation. Both necessity and chance are organically associated aspects of reality. The Greeks had symbolized them in two figures: one called *Ananke,* or necessity, a blind force; the other, *Tyche,* or chance. Both of these mythical figures, reflecting different aspects of reality, became objects of worship in cults. The question arose: which was supreme and ruled the world, *Ananke* (necessity) or *Tyche* (chance)?

These two sides of the same situation, or opposite poles of the same conception, are found together. How was the choice to be made between them? The one or the other was regarded as predominant in obedience to the specific social circumstances and class needs which were most coercive upon the given philosopher.

Epicurus lived in the period when the city-state was disintegrating, setting individuals free from their old ties and associations in the petty community. The new Alexandrian world empire was superseding the city-states and creating new types of relations between individuals and the society around them. The atomism of the Epicureans sought to take these new conditions into account and find a rational basis for the new social purposes. Their natural philosophy was closely akin to their ethics.

For example, the contradictory conception of the nature and functions of the gods, and the ambivalent attitude toward them held by the Epicureans, reflected the contradictory desires and demands arising from their own intermediate status in the social structure. The Epicureans sought to liberate men from domination by the gods and fear of them and fought to eliminate the arbitrary interference of supernatural forces in nature and society. They aimed to rid men's minds of superstition and to strike a blow at the use of religion as an instrument of mass subjection to aristocratic rule. This earned them the hatred of the idealist upholders of oligarchy and the traditional defenders of the religious associations.

Whereas, idealists like Plato advocated the self-sufficiency of the city-state, the Epicureans preached above all the self-sufficiency of the individual. The wise and happy man withdrew from public life, did not participate in political affairs, but "cultivated his own garden." This was a matter of deliberate choice in defiance of compulsion from without.

This prescription provided a general model for their conception of the atom, the gods, and the good life. The atoms which constituted the elements of the universe were impassive and impenetrable. The gods were equally idle and unconcerned with one another or with mankind. They lived in the spaces between the worlds and had no responsibility for what happened on earth. They, too, were composed of atoms, corporeal beings of human form but larger. They were not by nature immortal, although they could, like men, acquire immortality and preserve happiness by being watchful. There was no divine government of the universe, no divine providence for men, no prophecy. "The happiness of the Epicurean gods consists in large part of immunity from responsibilities. In this respect they resemble gentlemen of leisure, for whom all worldly occupations were sordid," observes DeWitt in *Epicurus and His Philosophy* (p. 277).

The self-sufficiency of the atoms and the deviation in their motion, the imperturbability of the gods and their cultivation of eternal bliss for themselves alone form a symmetrical complement to the self-sufficiency of the individual and the ideals of life recommended by Epicurus.

The peculiar characteristics of Epicureanism can best be grasped by contrasting them with the positions of Platonism. As the exponent of materialism, Epicurus was the sworn enemy of idealism. More than half of his forty authorized doctrines are flat contradictions of Platonism.

Epicurus scorned the Platonic conception that the universe was a work of art made by the gods to serve the needs and ends of mankind. The universe was the outcome of a material development proceeding from the movement of atoms in empty space with which the gods had nothing to do and which in fact created the gods themselves. There was no teleology in the Epicurean view of the cosmic process. The heavenly bodies had been created without any purpose in view and so had the organs of mankind. They were the result of haphazard adaptation, not divine foresight.

At the same time Epicurus sought to make a place

for the human being to react upon the environment, first laying the base by endowing the atom with an oblique motion, and then endowing mankind with a freedom of choice which sets him apart from and above the other animals. The atom and mankind were both free; chance, not necessity, had the upper hand.

For the classical idealists the model man was the citizen of the city-state who fully participated in all its public life. The perfect Epicurean was a very different personage. He felt no more responsibility for civic life than did the gods for the affairs of men. Since he could not dominate or direct the course of events either in nature or in politics, these being vested in external powers beyond control, he abstained from attempting the impossible.

There was, however, one sphere in which he could aspire to prevail. That was in the superintendence and control of his own life, especially his inner life. The precondition for this was withdrawal from public strife and the larger stage of events. The perfect Epicurean would not permit himself to be subservient either to the monarch or the mob, that is to say, turned his back equally upon the democratic and the oligarchic movements.

But he could improve his own self, plan his life within the compass of his household, and enjoy the company of like-minded associates. The individual's aim should be to avoid pain and achieve calm. For the idealists the goal of human endeavor was good citizenship attained by virtuous and enlightened conduct, knowledge of the ideal, and the pursuit of perfection through the divine forms. For the Epicurean the goal of human effort consisted in the pursuit of pleasure which was defined as the absence of pain.

The refined pursuit of pleasure recommended by Epicurus was far removed from the kind of life on the docks of Piraeus or in the turbulent agora of Athens. It was appropriate to people who can cultivate their private garden in peace. Nature is non-purposive but it has produced a creature in man capable of purpose. Pleasure is the end ordained by nature for man; men can attain that end by intelligent planning. There are different grades of pleasure. The pleasure of a sound body and mind is basic and can be enjoyed continually; others are superfluous and decorative. Pleasure is the health of mankind just as pain is its affliction. Pleasure is prior to virtue and more basic to life. The newborn infant can feel pleasure but cannot practice virtue. Virtue is chosen by adults for the sake of pleasure and not the other way around, as Plato and Aristotle held.

The Epicurean doctrine of pleasure insisted that the aim of human life is not self-denial, self-frustration or immolation but the improvement and perfection of its specific human qualities rid of superstition and fear. " I spit upon the beautiful and those who unreasonably adore it when it gives no pleasure," Epicurus vehemently cried. "As for me, it is to continuous pleasures that I invite you and not virtues that are empty and vain and offer but harassing hopes of reward." These continuous, stabilized pleasures were rational because they did not lead to loss of health and wealth and thereby bring pain.

Peace and security are the watchwords of Epicurean-

ism. His famous advice was: live without involve-
ment. Obviously this was not a counsel of active
participation in social life or resistance to its evils but
rather of passivity and conformity. It arose from a
sense that the social surroundings were hostile, uncontrollable and unchangeable and could be coped with
only by withdrawing from the contest of forces outside and barricading oneself within a citadel. But
this abstention did signify mute protest against their
predicament.

The Epicurean conception of the soul and body-soul
relationship was quite materialistic and in flat opposition to the Platonic conception. For the Epicureans the
soul was neither divine nor immortal. It was corporeal
in nature, being composed of smooth, spherical and
fine atoms, born at the same time as the body. The
body contains the soul as a vessel contains fluid. The
active capacities of the body are limited to sensation
while the soul possesses memory, intelligence and reason, although, as blushing, perspiring and trembling
indicate, the soul participates through the body in
sensation.

Still another key point on which Epicurus takes issue with Plato is on the nature of the Perfect Ideas
which Plato used to justify the rule of aristocracy. To
the Platonic view that justice was something absolute
and unchangeable, Epicurus opposed the Sophistic
notion that justice is relative and conditioned by
changing historical circumstances.

He stated: "There never has been an absolute justice,
only an agreement reached in social intercourse, differing from place to place and from time to time, for

preventing the injury of one man by another . . . All those elements in what is recognized at law as just possess that character in so far as they are proved by the necessities of social intercourse to be expedient, whether they are the same for everyone or not; and if a law turns out to be incompatible with the expediencies of social intercourse, it ceases to be just. And should the expediency expressed in the law correspond only for a time with that conception, nevertheless for the time it is just, so long as we do not trouble ourselves with empty phrases but look simply at the facts."

This is a devastating rejoinder to the conception of timeless standards of law and morality upheld by classical idealism.

In place of the civic loyalty to the aristocratic slave-state sanctified by eternal ideas, the Epicureans advocated individual sufficiency tempered by friendship on the one side and a philanthropic cosmopolitanism on the other. Although the Epicureans made no direct attack upon slavery or class society, or even upon the acquisition and enjoyment of wealth, they enjoined a love for mankind and tried to practice a sweet reasonableness toward others.

In his authorized doctrines Epicurus gave the following recipe on how to survive amidst troubled times: "That man has best forestalled the feeling of insecurity from outside who makes relations friendly where possible, where impossible, at least neutral, and where this is impossible, avoids contacts, and in all cases where it pays to do so arranges for dynastic support."

Epicurus practiced what he preached by confining teaching to his private estate in Athens instead of going about the city like Socrates and the Sophists. The house and garden of Epicurus was the site of his school. Administered by slaves, it was notable for one exceptional feature, the presence of certain women as equals and philosophers. These women were courtesans; among them was Leontion, the most distinguished courtesan of her time. She published a book attacking Theophrastus, the head of the Aristotelian Academy, who acknowledged that her manner of writing was both clever and good Attic Greek.

Epicurus was a teacher of moral conduct who not only disseminated ideas but founded a cult. His philosophy became a guide to everyday practice. He was revered almost as a god by his disciples. Although urging withdrawal from public life, the followers of Epicurus were evangelists who spread his creed from one end of the Graeco-Roman world to the other. They were released from the parochial limitations of the city-state idealists by the Macedonian monarchies and by their own individualistic and universalistic orientation. Anyone could join the Epicureans regardless of culture, race and status.

Epicureanism attained the status of a world philosophy, differing from the traditional folk religions and urban observances, opposed to Platonism and Stoicism among rival philosophies, and to the Eastern cults, Judaism and Christianity, among the world religions. Epicureanism made its greatest appeal not to the aristocrats or the masses, but to the intermediate layers, non-Greek as well as Greek. It was the first Greek philosophy to enter Roman Italy.

Its peculiar combination of conformism to the ruling powers and materialist criticism, deference to custom and innovation in religion made its outlook especially appealing to people who were caught between the ruling powers and the lower orders in the collapsing city-states under the Alexandrian and Roman empires and seeking a moral sanctuary from the disorders and dangers of the times.

The philosophers of the Epicurean sect who taught their members to turn inward were prototypes of the spiritual advisers and father-confessors of the Catholic Church who took charge of the spiritual lives of their clients and steered them toward happiness and virtue. They were rivals of the Stoics and later of the Christians. They flourished for seven centuries and disappeared as an organized movement along with the disintegration of Roman civilization, either dying out or becoming absorbed into the Christian faith.

The spirit of Epicureanism as a popular cult, rather than an esoteric philosophy, is expressed in the monuments of its disciples. Epicurean epitaphs are to be found engraved on gravestones throughout Italy, Gaul and Africa. "I was not, I was, I am not. I am unconscious of it." Another Epicurean sentiment is preserved in the Hebrew Bible in Ecclesiastes: "A living dog is better than a dead lion, for the living know that they shall die but the dead know not anything." This is a far cry from the Christian attitude where death is the gateway to divine and eternal life. For the Epicureans, death is annihilation of the individual and life the most precious of all boons, as it should be to materialists.

In the 2nd Century A.D. an old man in a small town in Asia Minor erected a monument inscribed with the teachings of Epicurus. On it he said that, after having experienced "the fullness of happiness," he wished to do something for the happiness of his own townsmen, for visitors, and even for those who were not yet born because "the whole universe is just one country and the whole earth just one household." This cosmopolitanism is a far cry from the city-state patriotism of the classical epoch in Greece.

Epicureanism not only developed into a world philosophy under the Alexandrian and Roman empires but it also inspired the most eminent single literary work of materialism in all antiquity, the poem of Lucretius on the nature of things. This supreme production marks the peak of materialist thought in the first phase of its evolution.

XVI. Materialism in Roman Civilization

GREECE WAS CONQUERED first by Macedonia in the 4th Century B.C. and then by Rome two centuries later. Neither of these military powers fostered any independent or original development of philosophy. The Roman cultivated classes took their philosophical ideas, like their alphabet, from the Greeks. The Greeks compensated for their political subordination by dominating their masters in the theoretical field.

This Roman tutelage to the more advanced and refined culture of Greece stands out in materialist theory which was disseminated in Rome largely through Epicurean influence. The Roman thinkers did not add anything essentially new to materialist philosophy. What they did was to elaborate the teachings of Epicurus and the Atomists and apply them to the situations and problems of their own times.

The most gifted exponent of Epicurean Atomism in

the Graeco-Roman world was the poet Lucretius. The epic which he wrote *On the Nature of Things* is the work of antiquity which is closest in spirit to modern materialism and which speaks most directly to us. It influenced the thinking of the renovators of science in the 17th Century and of Diderot and other materialists in the 18th Century and can still be studied with profit by every serious adherent to the materialist outlook.

Lucretius lived through the period in Roman history when the conflicts between the patricians and plebeians for control of the state came to a head and the Empire was acquired by incessant wars of conquest involving the extermination and enslavement of whole peoples. He himself refers to "the brutal business of war by sea and by land" and abroad and at home as an everyday affair. The bloody civil wars, marked by the execution or exile of the leaders of defeated factions, culminated in Caesar's military dictatorship, the Augustinian Empire, and the slave uprising led by Spartacus in 73 B.C.

Lucretius was a younger contemporary of Caesar and Cicero. The latter may have edited his poem and was certainly acquainted with it for he wrote in a letter to a friend early in 54 B.C.: "The poems of Lucretius are, as you describe them, marked by great brilliance of genius, but not by much art."

Lucretius explicitly based his work upon the teachings of Epicurus whom he venerated as the master of enlightenment and likened to a god. "Thee I follow, thou glory of the Greek people," he says, "and now fix my steps firmly in thy footprints and tread in them."

Two main schools of philosophy contended for

supremacy among the educated Romans: Epicureanism and Stoicism. The *De Rerum Natura* of Lucretius
was more than an eloquent exposition of Epicureanism
and a defense of materialism; it was a polemic against
Stoicism which carried forward in its own way the tradition of Greek idealism. The poem attacks most of
the main Stoic positions: their belief in a Divine Providence which rules the world; their conception of the
heavenly bodies as divine and self-moving; their doctrines of design and purpose in nature; their divine
necessity as opposed to human free will; their sponsor-
ing one finite spherical cosmos against the existence of
many worlds; their belief in the divinity and perfection
of the world, along with many of the social and ethical
ideas of the school.

The poem is above all an assault upon theology
and teleology, not in the theoretical formulations of
the philosophers but in its official and popular form
of the prevailing religious beliefs and practices. For
Lucretius, as for Voltaire, religious superstition was
public enemy No. 1. With Lucretius we can measure
the progress made by materialism since its birth in
Miletus. Thales implicitly set aside the gods as the
authors of the universe and the prime agency of
change. The Roman poet five centuries later totally
repudiates the gods as authors and agencies of anything; deprives them of all functions; sends them into
retirement; relentlessly chases them out of their last
hiding places in the operations of nature and society;
and castigates all those who preach or uphold the
power of the gods.

In those terrible and troubled times of transition

from the ancient Republic to the new world empire, the old Roman religious beliefs were waning especially amongst the upper classes. As Lucretius wrote: "Men were wandering hither and thither, and going far astray, groping for the way of life." Some turned to the new cults migrating from the East to Rome. "Even at this day, the sense of awe implanted in the heart of man by the observances of religion is raising new temples of gods over the whole earth."

The practice of divination, which had been performed in Greece by the priests at Delphi and other oracles, was the central feature of the Roman state religion in Lucretius' day. No important step could be taken without consulting the official soothsayers. The college of augurs served as the ultimate entrenchment of aristocratic rule against a dangerous candidate who might be close to election or a measure likely to pass of benefit to the plebeians. If an agrarian reform, for example, might compel nobles to disgorge misappropriated public lands, an augur would be found to say that he had consulted the sky and the gods had forbidden any public business that day, so that the Assembly had to be dissolved and could not act.

Many upper-class Romans who themselves had lost belief in the magic of augurs nevertheless insisted upon maintaining the imposture to dupe and police the people. Cicero, much like Plato before him, wrote: "Antiquity no doubt was deceived in many things, and has had to be corrected by time, by experience, or the spread of knowledge. And yet the reverence for augury and the college of augurs and the practice of augury must be kept up on account of the beliefs of the common people and for its great service to the state."

The Greek historian Polybius praises the Roman aristocracy for its adroit use of superstition in maintaining their power. "The foundation of Roman greatness," he asserted, "is superstition. This has been introduced into every aspect of their private and public life with every artifice to awe the imagination. For the masses in every state are unstable, full of lawless desires, irrational anger and violent passion. All that can be done is to hold them in check by fears of the unseen and similar shams. It was not for nothing but of deliberate design that the men of yore introduced to the masses notions about God and views on the after life."

Through their seers the rulers of Rome sought to keep the masses in terror by inculcating and fortifying fears for violating tabus which would be punished both now and in the after-life.

Lucretius was himself a patrician. In his poem he does not call upon an oppressed citizenry to throw off the burdens of aristocratic domination and extortion. But he does call upon his associates to cast off the fears induced by religious superstition and to stand erect as independent human beings uncowed by the dark and terrifying forces of the unknown and uncontrollable. As a materialist and a conscious rationalist who opposes science to religion, he urged his fellows to take the first step in their mental emancipation and to rely upon material forces and their own strength instead of succumbing to alien forces and prostrating themselves before the gods. Twice in his poems he declares that the old Greek natural philosophers, and not the oracle of Apollo at Delphi, ought to be revered as the fountainhead of truth.

Lucretius is a missionary bringing a message of liberation and salvation to the suffering humanity of his time. As one of his American translators, himself an excellent poet, William Ellery Leonard, remarked: "He talks like a man who knows how terrible it is to be bound, how magnificent to be free." Although the body of this thought is taken from Epicurus, its pervading spirit is far from calm; it is fierce, evangelical, militant. The viewpoint at which he has arrived seems to him the most precious possession which he has torn out of suffering and pain and which he burns to impart to others so that they, too, can be rid of torment.

He pays homage to Epicurus precisely because he braved the fabulous might of the gods and opened nature's secrets to men's sight. "When human life lay grovelling in all men's sight, crushed to the earth under the dead weight of superstition whose grim features loured menacingly upon mortals from the four quarters of the sky, a man of Greece was first to raise mortal eyes in defiance, first to stand erect and brave the challenge. Fables of the gods did not crush him, nor the lightning flash and the growling menace of the sky. Rather, they quickened his manhood, so that he, first of all men, longed to smash the constraining locks of nature's doors. The vital vigor of his mind prevailed. He ventured far out beyond the flaming ramparts of the world and voyaged in mind through infinity. Returning victorious, he proclaimed to us what can be and what cannot: how a limit is fixed to the power of everything and an immovable frontier post. Therefore superstition in its turn lies crushed beneath his feet, and we by his triumph are lifted to the skies."

Lucretius then turns the tables on the priests by insisting that, far from his discourse on the ultimate realities of the heavens and the gods being impious and sinful, religion itself is the mother of vicious deeds such as the sacrifice of the virgin Iphigenia by her father's hand. He exhorts his patrician friend Memmius not to backslide by surrendering to the bloodcurdling phantoms of the soothsayers but to remain a firm follower of the light of reason.

It may appear anomalous that Lucretius, the materialist, invokes the aid of Venus as the guiding power of the universe at the opening of his exposition of atomism. But the poet aims to celebrate through the goddess the creative energies of nature which give birth to all things, all living creatures, the flowers, the birds, and love. This materialist looks upon nature not as a dead mechanism but as the everlasting and inexhaustible source of all creation. This conception of nature as the fount of creativity, which is an essential element of a rounded materialist outlook, will be met again at the revival of materialism with Bruno in the 16th Century.

Lucretius knew that true knowledge of natural phenomena helped to banish superstitions. "As children in blank darkness tremble and start at everything, so we in broad daylight are oppressed at times by fears as baseless as those horrors which children imagine coming upon them in the dark. This dread and darkness of the mind cannot be dispelled by the sunbeams, the shining shafts of day, but only by an understanding of the outwards and inner workings of nature," he writes.

The major weapon Lucretius consciously wielded against the official religion is his materialist explanation of the universe. The first two books of his poem present the basic principles of the atomic view of the physical world. The next two books deal with mankind. The second book expounds the nature of the soul and the way it is connected with the body, giving proofs of the mortality of the soul. It is interesting—and ironic—to note that whereas the idealist Socrates invokes the immortality of the soul to banish fear of death, the materialist Lucretius points to its mortality for the same purpose.

The third book takes up sensation, thought and biological functions. Lucretius, like Epicurus, believed in the primacy of the senses in experience and knowledge. He used his own senses masterfully for these purposes. He had none of the idealist disparagement of the body and the senses which goes hand in hand with the exaltation of pure reason and revelation in the form of intuition as the sole source of true knowledge. His reliance upon the senses can be seen in the vivid images and illustrations scattered throughout his pages and by the way he turns to direct observation, guided and promoted by analytical reasoning, for proof of the truth of his atomic theory.

It is sometimes said that the atomic theory of the ancient materialists was no more than a lucky guess which had no scientific foundation in their activities or thinking but by coincidence turned out to be an anticipation of reality. It is true that speculation as well as observation played a part in the formulation of their atomic theory and often speculation went wide of the mark. But it is not the unavoidable misses of the Atomists but their hits—and above all their hit at the center of the target—that have to be accounted for. A study of the poem of Lucretius makes it clear that the views of the Atomists were drawn from close and critical-minded examination of the processes of nature. From the outward manifestations of nature that came to their notice they deduced the inner operations of atomic elements. In the slow diminution of objects by attrition, such as a paving stone or the kissed hand of a statue, in the minute character of many visible objects, like dust in the sunbeams, in the physical effects of the invisible winds, of odors, and of heat, Lucretius sees manifest demonstrations of the movements of small particles and the formation, transformation and reformation of all things. "Nature," he concludes, "works through the agency of invisible bodies."

Although on a far more rudimentary level of social and scientific development, this method and its conclusions is not fundamentally different from the procedures of modern science in discovering and explaining such a phenomenon as the movement of molecules which Brown first discerned in the suspension of certain liquids and Einstein explained in theoretical terms. To be sure, Lucretius did not engage in planned laboratory experiments with controls and repeated verifications under changed conditions; these more precise methods were added much later to scientific research. But within the compass of the scientific techniques of his time he gave reasonable and verifiable interpretations of natural phenomena.

For example, present-day scientists have still to solve the problem of rain formation; it is thought that rain comes from sea-salt in the atmosphere. This is precisely what Lucretius said 2,000 years ago: "We must reckon also with the fact that nature causes a constant stream of particles to rise up from the whole ocean, as shown when clothes hung up on the shore receive an accession of moisture. This suggests that the clouds may also be swollen, in no small measure, by an exhalation from the ocean's briny surge; for its moisture is of a kindred quality."

Book Five deals with the earth and its history, describing the nature and formation of the world, the emergence of life, and the development of human society. The sixth and final part of his uncompleted work concerns itself with meteorology and geology and ends with a treatment of epidemics and the great plague at Athens during the Peloponnesian War depicted by the historian Thucydides. In this section Lucretius discloses his kinship with the Hippocratic school of medicine by ascribing certain diseases to variations in the air and climate.

Lucretius strives to give a clear, connected and comprehensive explanation of the principal phenomena encountered in all these domains of reality. His materialist consistency is admirable. As Farrington well says: "In no other single work in the whole of antiquity, and I think I might add in the modern world either, is there to be found a comparable effort to muster all the phenomena of nature and history as joint witnesses to a unified view of things." A view unified, we might add, by an unyielding materialism.

Lucretius set forth many fruitful ideas which point the way to modern science: matter as composed of tiny invisible particles; of atoms moving at infinitely swift and brief motion; of the vast stretches of space and time; of the reign of law throughout the cosmos; of the infinite diversity of things.

One of the most instructive sections, the second part of the fifth book, sets forth his views on the origin of life and the progress of society. This brief sketch of civilization is one of antiquity's greatest contributions to historical materialism. It seeks to eliminate the action of providence from the domain of human history and to search for intelligible causes of progress in the material conditions of the animal and human environment rather than in the will and reason of man or the intervention of the gods.

Lucretius presents a theory of organic and social evolution, although he does not touch on the origin and alteration of species. After this world was formed not by the gods who are remote and unconcerned but by the coming together of atoms, "the new-born earth first flung up herbs and shrubs. Next in order it engendered the various breeds of mortal creatures." In time the fruitful earth, mother nature, grew old and sterile, ceased to propagate, and then living beings began to propagate themselves.

Primitive man was not a producer but a food gatherer. He did not have fire, clothing or houses but dwelt in mountain caves and mated promiscuously. He avoided the more dangerous wild animals and hunted others with sticks and stones.

Civilization began after men got fire, either through a conflagration caused by lightning or the ignition of branches of trees rubbed together by the wind, and acquired skin-clothing and huts. Man and wife began to mate permanently and to watch over their joint progeny. Neighbors formed mutual alliances and created society.

His notions on the origin of language avoided teleological explanation. Tongues were not designed for speaking but speech originated in society as a by-product of tongues. Just as animals and birds express a variety of emotions by distinct sounds, so men used different sounds to designate different things until by agreement language was established.

"As time went by, men learned to change the old way of life by fire and other inventions, instructed by those of outstanding ability and mental energy. Kings began to found cities and establish citadels for their own safeguard and refuge. They parcelled out cattle and lands, giving to each according to his looks, his strength and his ability . . . Later came the invention of property and the discovery of gold which speedily robbed the strong and the handsome of their preeminence." That is, wealth became more important than personal worth.

In the envious and ambitious society that resulted, monarchy was overthrown and anarchy prevailed. Anarchy in turn was replaced by constitutional government where wrongdoers were checked by magistrates and laws. Religion then arose to torment men with dread because men mistakenly believed that the gods they envision rule and direct the universe.

The first lessons in metallurgy were given when forest fires melted gold, silver, lead, copper and iron and suggested to men the forging of weapons and instruments. Previous to his knowledge of metals, man's weapons and implements had been hands, nails, teeth, branches torn from trees, flame and fire. Lucretius then takes up the technical development of warfare, weaving, agriculture, music, navigation, poetry and writing.

In this remarkable theory of social evolution nature is not simply the mother but the tutor of mankind. The sun teaches men how to cook; the birds and the winds how to make music; lightning how to create fire; forest fires how to smelt metals. By imitating the ways of nature and enlisting its powers, mankind increases its productive and mental capacities and lifts itself to civilization.

Lucretius rightly attached great importance to the key technical inventions in the progress of mankind. And he saw that history has its laws. He concluded: "Ships and tillage, walls, laws, arms, roads, dress and all such like things, all the prizes, all the elegancies too of life without exception, poems, pictures, and the chiselling of fine-wrought statues, all these things practiced together with the acquired knowledge of the untiring mind taught men by slow degrees as they advanced on the way step by step. Thus time by degrees brings each several things forth before men's eyes and reason raises it up into the light of day; for things must be brought to light one after another and in due

order in the different arts, until these have reached
their highest point of development."

The knowledge and theory of the Greeks and Romans on the development of society had advanced by
degrees from the Ionians until it climbed to the top-
most peak in this outline by Lucretius. He summarized
the method and teachings of the materialists on these
problems. There was to be nothing comparable in the
science of sociology until the Arabian scholar Ibn
Khaldun thirteen centuries later.

Following the passionate and reasoned argument
of Lucretius from the opening apostrophe to its abrupt
end, the sympathetic reader is moved to exclaim:
"What a proud thing it is to be a materialist and not
to flinch and falter before the dark recesses in nature
and the blind forces of society which beset mankind,
betray, hobble and overthrow him!" As Vergil, himself
inspired by Lucretius, wrote: "Happy is he who knows
the causes of things."

But there are undertones of sadness and pessimism
in the poem. Lucretius believed that the existing world
was in its declining phase and coming to its end. He
is said to have gone mad and committed suicide before finishing his masterpiece. Historically, the Roman
Republic was coming to its end amidst the most ago-
nizing convulsions and the Empire was taking its
place.

The end of the road for ancient materialism was also
in sight. Although Lucretius, the poet, won the admiration of his fellow Romans, he did not inspire any
further advance in philosophy. He remained isolated,
His ideas were the last brilliant glow of the material-

ism of antiquity which was soon to sink below the horizon. The fundamental outlook of materialism proved incompatible with both the further development and the decline of Roman civilization. The religions he fought sprang forth in fresh forms, and helped to eclipse the light of critical reason and materialist science which he tended.

Fortunately, the poem of Lucretius and its view of the world were to survive in a single copy to inspire the reawakening of materialism in the 17th Century. It remains to our day the incomparable statement of the noblest and truest ideas bequeathed from the Greeks and the Romans.

> *Here rolls*
> *The large verse of Lucretius, who raised*
> *His index-finger and did strike the face*
> *Of fleeting Time, leaving a scar of thought*
> *The rain of ages shall not wash away.*

▤ Lucian

BEFORE LEAVING THE company of the materialists in Graeco-Roman times, one person should not be slighted. That is Lucian. Lucretius was a philosophical poet; Lucian was a satirist, a moralist, a caustic critic of Graeco-Roman customs. With Lucretius materialism in antiquity culminates in a magnificent affirmation of itself, vindicating its potency and validity against religion, Stoic idealism and skepticism.

Two centuries later Lucian shows us the philosophic tradition of Greece and Rome in disintegration and collapse, unsure of itself and its future. With Lucian philosophy appears lost in a maze of contradictions after treading false paths which lead nowhere. There is no exit upon any highroad which can bring mankind to truth, enlightenment, certitude. However, this decadence of thought does not seem to Lucian any reason for despair. If religion is preposterous and philosophy futile, he still feels, like Montaigne, a sturdy spiritual and intellectual support in an enlightened common-sense guided by critical reasoning, sprinkled with skepticism, and seasoned with dashes of cynicism.

Lucian was a cosmopolitan Syrian, born about 120 A.D., who became a wandering lecturer by profession. At his death he held high office in the Imperial Treasury in Egypt. The Mediterranean world of the 2nd Century had become Romanized, Hellenized, pacified, unified and, in its upper circles, luxurious and literate.

Although he wrote on painting, drawing, a trip to the moon and a diversity of subjects, his principal productions were short satiric dialogues, mocking the gods, deriding the living through the dead, exposing religious impostors from downright quacks to sincere believers, exploding the pretentions of various schools of philosophy. He recalls Diderot in his use of satire as a weapon against falsehood and sham. Engels called him "the Voltaire of antiquity."

One of his outstanding traits, an acute commentator has observed, was "a passionate sympathy for the lower classes, for the millions who lived on farms and in tenement houses, artisans, laborers, sailors, harlots. The injustice of human life haunts him. He drags in the slums, even in his burlesque." Lucian was a self-made man of poor parentage who had decided to apprentice himself at fifteen to his mother's uncle, a stone-carver. After having been beaten for accidentally breaking a piece of marble, he ran away from his master and prepared himself for a writing and speaking career. The young footloose Lucian became familiar with poverty and neglect.

In Lucian's Hades, society is turned upside down and the roles of the classes are reversed. The rich and the powerful become penniless and despised; the common people enact legislation against the powers that were.

His wrathful attitude toward the rich is seen in one of his *Dialogues of the Dead* where the popular assembly of Hades passes the following decree against the Plutocrats: "Whereas the Plutocrats perpetuate a number of inequities in life, by plunder, by violence, and in every way utterly despising the Poor, be it enacted by the Senate and the People that, when they die, their bodies undergo punishment, just as do those of other worthless people, but that the *souls* be sent up above again into life, and enter into asses, until they have, in such state, passed through two hundred and fifty thousand years, becoming asses from generation to generation, and carrying heavy burdens, and driven by the poor laborers; and after that period, that it be permitted them finally to die."

Lucian addresses the Gout in a mocking vein. "O, Goddess! who hatest the Poor, and are the sole subduer of wealth, who knowest how to live 'well' at all times, thou delightest to be supported on strange feet, and knowest how to wear shoes of felt, and ointments are a care to thee. Thee, too, garlands delight, and the liquor of the Ausonian Bacchus. But these things never exist, at any time, for the Poor. And, therefore, thou fleeest from the threshold of poverty, that has no gold, and art delighted, on the other hand, in coming to the feet of wealth."

Religion is another target of his wit. Whereas Lucretius assails superstition, Lucian ridicules it. He lets loose his shafts not only against religious quacks but against the gods. In his *Dialogues of the Gods* he transforms Olympus, their abode, into a bourgeois household where jealous Hera squabbles with her husband Zeus over his infidelities with boys as well as with women.

In another dialogue he describes a panicky council where the gods, like threatened aristocrats, are concerned about being deposed from office. The alarmed Zeus tells the assembly, which includes barbarian along with Greek gods, that they are likely to die of starvation because the sacrifices offered to them are so scanty and scrawny. He complains that a ship captain who had promised a banquet when his ship was heading for the rocks, in fact offered only a single cock when he had sixteen gods to entertain; that was "an old bird afflicted with catarrh—and half a dozen grains of frankincense: those were all mildewed so that they frizzled out on the embers, hardly giving enough smoke to tickle the nostrils."

Zeus blames the teachings of the atheists for these slim pickings. "As I was engaged in these thoughts, I reached the Portico, and there I found a large crowd of men vociferating. I judged correctly that there were philosophers of the militant variety, and I stopped to listen. The bone of contention was ourselves. Damis the atheist—the reptile—was maintaining that we did not exist. Timocles was on our side. He illustrated the orderly and discerning character of our government and extolled our providence. But he was exhausted and quite husky; the majority were inclining toward irreligion. I saw how much was at stake, and ordered night to come and broke up the meeting."

Then, in the person of Momus, the god of Raillery, the voice of Lucian himself, his sympathy for the oppressed flashes forth and he shows the social sources of his aversion to the gods. "I swear to you," Momus says, "that we need not blame the philosophers for the prevalence of atheism. Why, what can one expect of men when they see all life today topsy-turvy—the good neglected, pining in poverty, disease, and slavery; detestable scoundrels honored, rolling in wealth and ordering their betters about; temple robbers undetected and unpunished; the innocent constantly crucified and bastinadoed? With this evidence it is only natural that they should conclude against our existence."

If Lucian makes fun of the gods and their false prophets, he places no confidence in any of the philosophical sects, although he feels closest to the Epicureans. All the sects contradict one another, he contends; none possesses or teaches the truth. In one of his philosophic dialogues he quizzes a friend, Herotimus, who had studied philosophy for twenty years and become a Stoic because it was the most popular creed. Yet he had still not attained either happiness or truth. Herotimus fails to convince Lucian of the rightness of his choice and exclaims in exasperation: "Why, you will not accept anything I say."

"On the contrary, my dear sir, it is you who will not say anything I accept."

Toward the end of their discussion Lucian, through the pseudonym of Lycinus, says: "I know just as little as before which traveller to trust, for each of them has travelled only one way. Whether he tells the truth or not, I have no means of knowing; that he has attained some end, and seen some city, I may perhaps allow; but whether he saw the right one, that is as yet undecided."

His friend replies: "It is just your way; you want to crow over me; you detest philosophy—I cannot tell why—and poke fun at philosophers."

"Herotimus, I cannot tell you what truth is so well

as wise people like you and your professor; but one thing I do know about it, and that is that it is not pleasant to the ear; falsehood is far more esteemed; it is prettier and therefore pleasanter; while Truth, conscious of its purity, blurts out downright remarks, and offends people. Here is a case of it; even you are offended with me for having discovered (with your assistance) how this matter really stands, and shown that our common object is hard of attainment. Suppose you had been in love with a statue and hoped to win it, under the impression that it was human, and I had realized that it was bronze or marble, and given you a friendly warning that your passion was hopeless—you might just as well have thought I was your enemy then, because I would not leave you prey to extravagant and impracticable delusions."

Herotimus: "Oh, come, now! Not one of them right?"

"I cannot tell. Do you think it impossible that they may all be deluded and the truth something which none of them has yet found?"

With this question mark over all philosophies the curtain falls upon the materialism of the Graeco-Roman world. Lucian's mocking laughter over the gods and his skepticism toward the philosophers indicates how far religion had fallen in the esteem of educated men since the days of Homer and how enfeebled philosophy had become since its birth in Ionia and its maturity in Athens.

In Homer the gods and the fates are all-powerful in governing the universe and the destiny of men. In Lucian they are butts of ridicule whom a reasonable person will only despise and scorn.

In Ionia philosophy rises up as the rival of religion and with the Atomists comes to supersede it as an explanation of the universe and history. With Lucian this rational certainty solidly based on empirical evidence gives way to agnosticism and skepticism. The philosophic sects offer no better or surer guide to the truth of things than their religious rivals. The twilight of the gods likewise enshrouds the philosophers.

Rational thought together with materialist philosophy had arrived at a blind alley and came to a dead stop. In subsequent Roman civilization and the antique world it could find no foothold for further progress. The social forces in the urban centers which had nurtured philosophy from its infancy to its young manhood had spent their last ideological resources. There were no up-and-coming classes in the declining slave society to relight and carry forward the flickering torch of rationalism. With Lucian it spurted into a final fireworks of light—and then went out.

XVII. The Eclipse of Materialism

WE HAVE NOW FINISHED OUR review of the history of materialism in Graeco-Roman times from the 6th Century B.C. to the 2nd Century A.D. This was the first stage in the development of the materialist outlook, its springtime, its youth.

We have seen how philosophy originated in the commercial centers of Ionia in the 6th Century as a materialist departure from religious traditions; how this primitive naturalism rose to its theoretical height in the dialectical insights of Heraclitus; became entangled in insoluble contradictions brought forth by the Pythagoreans and Eleatics; recovered its ground and renewed itself on a higher level in the Atomism of Leucippus and Democritus; how with the Sophists and Socrates philosophy split into increasingly divergent viewpoints which came into ever deeper conflict with each other; and thereafter moved along the two opposing paths of idealism and materialism which inter-

sected and interacted upon each other; how materialism survived the criticism of the classical idealists and
reconstituted itself in the doctrines of Epicurus, which
found their finest and fullest expression in the epic of
Lucretius; and finally how both philosophy and its
materialist tendency dissolved into the mocking skepticism of Lucian which foretold its eclipse in antiquity.

What did materialist thought accomplish in this
primary phase of its development?

1. In *physics,* the knowledge of nature, the ancient
materialists explained the universe as an independently
existing reality in constant change, operating according to its own laws and with an atomic structure of
matter.

2. In *logic,* the theory of knowledge, they regarded
sensation as the primary factor in acquiring acquaintance with the external world. "All the senses are heralds
of truth" (Epicurus). Reasoning leading to scientific
knowledge depended upon the materials provided in
the first place by sensory experience.

3. In *sociology,* the science of society, they viewed
history as the work of man imitating nature, utilizing
its ways and means to satisfy his material needs and
then developing civilization by the improvement of his
own skills.

4. In *ethics,* the theory of morality, they put forward a secular and relativistic conception of moral
conduct and its changing standards. They created the
foundations of a rational humanism as a guide to
the good life on earth.

All these theories had pronounced inconsistencies
and great gaps owing to the immature state of society

and science. The ideas of the early materialists were simplified, rough-hewn and awkward, like the products of all pioneering efforts. But they were immensely creative and essentially correct, supplying the foundations upon which all subsequent materialist thought was to build.

The careers of philosophy and its materialist expression were bound up with the development and disintegration of Graeco-Roman civilization and its component classes.

Strains of idealism and materialism were intertwined to one degree or another in all the ancient philosophers. But the idealist tendency, as a rationalized reconstruction of religious views and an ideological instrument of patrician domination, corresponded to the specific world outlook, political requirements, and social-psychological characteristics of the Greek and Roman urban aristocracies, slaveholders and wealthy landed proprietors. The general thought of these sections of the ruling classes was, however, influenced both positively and negatively by the conditions of urban culture and by the interests, ideas and movements of the manufacturers, merchants, money-lenders, shipowners and craftsmen. These opposing social forces interpenetrated one another. This can be seen not only in certain positive doctrines of the idealists but in the very fact that they had to adopt the rational form and logical methods of philosophy as the mode of expression of their class needs in place of the mythological material of the local cults which adequately served the old monarchies.

For example, even though the patrician idealists

regarded hand workmanship as vulgar *(banausic)*, Plato designated the Creator as craftsman *(demiurgos)*. The social productive category of the specialized workman whose functions he disesteemed was used for the supreme power in the universe.

The materialist tendency, on the other hand, was the distinctive outlook of the historically new and socially dynamic forces in the Greek city-states born and sustained by their far-flung trade, industry, banking and government interests: the merchants, manufacturers, shipowners, along with sizeable bodies of artisans, miners, and maritime workers. Their thought in turn was subjected to the influences and pressures exerted from above by the aristocrats and from below by the discontented peasants, soldiers, plebeians, foreigners, freedmen, and even slaves in their city-states.

Neither of these two philosophic tendencies were world views characteristic of the plebeian classes or the slaves who were the producers of their wealth. Philosophy throughout antiquity remained the privileged possession and product of the educated upper orders who had the leisure, opportunity and incentive to theorize about the problems of nature, society, and the human mind. Throughout class society, and above all this phase of it, theory has not been an activity of the whole people but only a small segment of it. In the main the producing masses lacked the most elementary conditions for intellectual life or else they had to feed intellectually upon the old religions or the new cults and mysteries.

However, the commoners were not all on the same level in their social positions or in their living, working, or civic conditions and thereby not all of one type in their activities, ideas and general outlooks. If the bulk of the lower classes subsisted intellectually on magic, religion, or practical common sense, in so far as they held wide views of the world, the more alert and enlightened among them in the cities and on the ships inclined toward and were powerful social supports for the empirical, materialist and naturalistic thinkers. For the most part they found the ideological spokesmen for their points of view, as they did their political leaders, in radical representatives of the upper orders who had the ways and means of performing speculative and scientific work. The democratic plebeians did not develop an exclusive class ideology and outlook in philosophic terms; they shared their most enlightened ideas with other, more favored strata from the Ionian naturalists through the Atomists to Lucian.

This anomalous state of affairs, whereby one class performed ideological functions for another, arose from the very nature of the slave state which wedged the plebeians in between a servile class and a plutocratic aristocracy. Under such conditions the plebeians could not find a way clear to create a secular ideology of their own any more than did the slaves beneath them. At the same time neither the mercantile nor the landed classes could propel philosophy further either along idealist or materialist lines. Philosophy foundered in the midst of these social contradictions. The slave structure which had placed its stigma and limitations upon ancient thought from its beginnings was the ultimate cause of its undoing. Having erected impassable barriers to the expansion of thought beyond its own framework, the decaying slave economy of Greece and Rome eventually undermined the foundations of the ideologies developed during its prime. Philosophy was a victim of the exhaustion of the classical slave civilizations.

It was not the only cultural casualty. The progress of natural science stopped together with that of materialism. The last great figures in ancient science, Ptolemy, the astronomer, and Galen, the physician, both lived in the 2nd Century A.D. After their time the major scientific works of the West were commentaries and compilations. When the Moslems invaded the Mediterranean basin during the 7th Century, they found only the documentary relics and traditions of ancient learning. The creative activity had long ceased.

*   *   *

We can trace a persistent development and consistent tradition of materialist thought in the intellectual circles of Greece and Rome from 6th Century Ionia to Lucretius and Lucian eight centuries later. All these thinkers had affiliations with one another and opposed themselves to the gods and the idealist defenders of theology and teleology.

After Lucretius the continuity was broken; the tradition snapped. As Farrington pithily observed: materialism, after making the most valiant fight, became the defeated party in the thought of antiquity. Debased types of idealism like Stoicism, Neo-Platonism or Neo-

Aristotelianism thrust it from the arena. Then Christianity triumphed as the state religion and suppressed materialism for many centuries. Theology drove materialism underground and made philosophy its serf. The Christian dogma of the Fall of Man and his redemption through the grace of God and his only begotten Son supplanted the Greek materialist doctrine of the rise of man through the aid of natural means and his own collective efforts, best expounded by Lucretius.

It required radically different historical conditions and a far more advanced technology and social setting before materialism could return from exile in the Western world and rise to its feet again. But that was 1,300 years ahead.

Nothing throws more light on the degradation of philosophy and the plight of materialism than to contrast the materialist panorama of Lucretius and the sunny rationalist satire of Lucian with the sickly mysticism of the Neo-Platonists and the religious apologetics of the early Church fathers. It is like the difference between high noon in a flowering meadow and a foggy evening in a miasmic swampland.

But if materialism was banished and in chains for centuries, it was not totally lost. To some extent it found refuge among the Arabian cultures in the intervening centuries. When it came back 1,300 years later to Western Europe, materialism was to battle religion and idealism with stronger weapons than it wielded during antiquity and make further imperishable contributions to scientific thought, the advancement of social life and the enlightenment of progressive mankind.

Works Cited in this Book

ANDREWES, A., *The Greek Tyrants,* London, 1956.

ARISTOTLE, *Basic Works,* ed. Richard McKeon, New York, 1941.

BAILEY, C., *The Greek Atomists and Epicurus,* Oxford, 1928. *Epicurus, the Extant Remains,* Oxford, 1926.

BARKER, E., *Greek Political Theory: Plato and his Predecessors,* London, 1947.

BHABHA, H. J., "The Peaceful Uses of Atomic Energy," *Bulletin of the Atomic Scientists,* Vol. XI, No. 8, Chicago, 1955.

BONNARD, A., *Greek Civilization,* New York, 1959.

BOYLE, R., *Philosophical Works,* ed. P. Shaw, Vol. I, London, 1725.

BREASTED, J. H., *The Conquest of Civilization,* New York, 1938.

BREHIER, E., *Histoire de la Philosophie,* Vol. I, Paris, 1928.

BURNET, J., *Early Greek Philosophy,* London, 1920.

BURY, J. B., *The Ancient Greek Historians,* London, 1909.

COCHRANE, C. N., *Thucydides and the Science of History,* London, 1929.

CORNFORD, F. M., *From Religion to Philosophy,* London, 1912. *Principium Sapientiae: The Origins of Greek Philosophical Thought,* Cambridge, 1952.

CORNFORTH, M., *Science Versus Idealism,* London, 1955.

DE WITT, N. W., *Epicurus and his Philosophy,* Minneapolis, 1954.

DRACHMANN, A. B., *Atheism in Pagan Antiquity,* Copenhagen, 1922.

DUNHAM, A. G., *The History of Miletus,* London, 1915.

DURANT, W. J., *The Life of Greece,* New York, 1939.

ENCYCLOPEDIA OF RELIGION AND ETHICS, ed. J. Hastings, Vol. VIII, New York, 1955.

ENGELS, F., *Ludwig Feuerbach and the Outcome of German Classical Philosophy,* New York, 1941.

FARRINGTON, B., *Greek Science,* London, 1949.

FREEMAN, K., *The Pre-Socratic Philosophers,* Oxford, 1946.

GODLEY, A. D., *Socrates and Athenian Society,* London, 1896.

GOMPERZ, T., *Greek Thinkers,* London, 1912.

HEGEL, G., *History of Philosophy,* Vol. I, London, 1892.

HERODOTUS, *Histories,* New York, 1958.

HOLBACH, Baron d', *The System of Nature,* Boston, 1889.

HUME, D., *Philosophical Works,* Vol. IV, Boston, 1854.

JARDÉ, A., *The Formation of the Greek People,* New York, 1926.

KAUTSKY, K., *Foundations of Christianity,* New York, 1925.

LANGE, F. A., *The History of Materialism,* New York, 1925.

LEIBNIZ, G. W., *Philosophical Papers and Letters,* ed. L. E. Loemker, Vol. II, Chicago, 1956.

LILLEY, S., *Men, Machines and History,* London, 1948.

LUCIAN, The Loeb Classical Library, 8 Vols., London, 1913.

LUCRETIUS, *The Nature of the Universe,* tr. R. E. Latham, Harmondsworth, 1951.

MASSON, J., *The Atomic Theory of Lucretius,* London, 1884. *Lucretius, Epicurean and Poet,* London, 1909.

MILLIKAN, R. A., *The Electron,* Chicago, 1917.

PLEKHANOV, G., *In Defense of Materialism,* London, 1947.

RIVAUD, A., *Le Probleme de Devenir et la Notion de la Matière dans la Philosophie Grecque, depuis les Origines jusqu'a Théophraste,* Paris, 1906.

ROBIN, L., *Greek Thought and the Origins of the Scientific Spirit,* New York, 1928.

ROSS, W. D., *Aristotle,* London, 1923.

SAMBURSKY, S., *The Physical World of the Greeks,* New York, 1956.

STACE, W. T., *A Critical History of Greek Philosophy,* New York, 1956.

THOMSON, G., *Aeschylus and Athens,* London, 1941. *Studies in Ancient Greek Society,* Vol. I, New York, 1949. *Studies in Ancient Greek Society,* Vol. II: *The First Philosophers,* New York, 1955.

THUCYDIDES, *History of the Peloponnesian War,* tr. R. Warner, London, 1954.

UNTERSTEINER, M., *The Sophists,* New York, 1954.

VOCABULAIRE TECHNIQUE ET CRITIQUE DE LA PHILOSOPHIE, ed. A. Lalande, Paris, 1951.

VOEGELIN, E., *Order and History*, Vol. II, Louisiana, 1957.

WINSPEAR, A. D., *The Genesis of Plato's Thought*, New York, 1956.

WRIGHT, R., *Black Power*, New York, 1954.

Index

FURTHER READING

The Communist Manifesto
Karl Marx, Frederick Engels

Founding document of the modern working-class movement, published in 1848. Explains how capitalism arose as a specific stage in the economic development of class society and how it will be superseded by socialism through worldwide revolutionary action by the working class. Booklet $2.50

Socialism: Utopian and Scientific
Frederick Engels

Modern socialism is not a doctrine, Engels explains, but a working-class movement growing out of the establishment of large-scale capitalist industry and its social consequences. Booklet $3.00

The Origin of the Family, Private Property, and the State
Frederick Engels, introduction by *Evelyn Reed*

How the emergence of class-divided society gave rise to repressive state bodies and family structures that protect the property of the ruling layers and enable them to pass along wealth and privilege. Engels discusses the consequences for working people of these class institutions—from their origins until modern times. $16.95

The History of the Russian Revolution
Leon Trotsky

The social, economic, and political dynamics of the first socialist revolution. The story is told by one of the revolution's principal leaders writing from exile in the early 1930s, with these historic events still fresh in his mind. Also available in Russian. Unabridged edition, 3 vols. in one. 1,358 pp. $35.95

AVAILABLE FROM PATHFINDER

The Changing Face of U.S. Politics

Working-Class Politics and the Trade Unions
Jack Barnes

A handbook for workers coming into the factories, mines, and mills, as they react to the uncertain life, ceaseless turmoil, and brutality of capitalism in the closing years of the twentieth century. It shows how millions of workers, as political resistance grows, will revolutionize themselves, their unions, and all of society. $19.95

February 1965: The Final Speeches

Malcolm X

Speeches from the last three weeks of Malcolm X's life, presenting the accelerating evolution of his political views. A large part is material previously unavailable, with some in print for the first time. The inaugural volume in Pathfinder's selected works of Malcolm X. $17.95

Cosmetics, Fashions, and the Exploitation of Women

Joseph Hansen, Evelyn Reed, and Mary-Alice Waters

How big business promotes cosmetics to generate profits and perpetuate the oppression of women. In her introduction, Mary-Alice Waters explains how the entry of millions of women into the workforce during and after World War II irreversibly changed U.S. society and laid the basis for a renewed rise of struggles for women's equality. $12.95

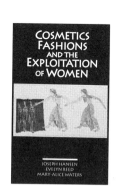

WORKS BY GEORGE NOVACK

Understanding History
Marxist Essays
How did capitalism arise? Why has this exploitative system exhausted its potential? Why is revolutionary change fundamental to human progress? $15.95

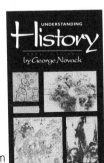

An Introduction to the Logic of Marxism
Marxism is dialectical, Novack explains. It considers all phenomena in their development, in their transition from one state to another. And it is materialist, explaining the world as matter in motion that exists prior to and independently of human consciousness. $12.95

America's Revolutionary Heritage
Marxist Essays
Explanatory essays on Native Americans, the first American revolution, the Civil War, the rise of industrial capitalism, and the first wave of the fight for women's rights. $21.95

Democracy and Revolution
The limitations and advances of various forms of democracy in class society, from its roots in ancient Greece through its rise and decline under capitalism. Discusses the emergence of Bonapartism, military dictatorship, and fascism, and how democracy will be advanced under a workers and farmers regime. $18.95

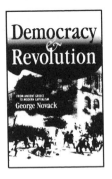

Polemics in Marxist Philosophy $19.95
Humanism and Socialism $13.95
Empiricism and Its Evolution $13.95
Pragmatism versus Marxism
An Appraisal of John Dewey's Philosophy $19.95

—————————————————— AVAILABLE FROM PATHFINDER